For Better or For Worse? School Finance Reform in California

• • •

Jon Sonstelie
Eric Brunner
Kenneth Ardon

2000

PUBLIC POLICY INSTITUTE OF CALIFORNIA

Library of Congress Cataloging-in-Publication Data
Sonstelie, Jon, 1946–
   For better or for worse? : school finance reform in California /
Jon Sonstelie, Eric Brunner, Kenneth Ardon.
     p. cm.
  Includes bibliographical references.
  ISBN: 1-58213-018-3
    1. Education—California—Finance. 2. Education—
Law and legislation—California. 3. Government aid to
education—California. I. Brunner, Eric, 1964– II. Ardon,
Kenneth, 1967– III. Title.

LB2826.C2 S65 2000
379.1'222'09794—dc21   00-020497

Research publications reflect the views of the authors and do not
necessarily reflect the views of the staff, officers, or Board of
Directors of the Public Policy Institute of California.

Foreword

In the late 1960s, Arthur Wise's *Rich Schools, Poor Schools: The Promise of Equal Educational Opportunity* prepared the legal ground for three decades of school finance reform. In that book, Wise argued that disparities in school expenditures arising from differences in wealth or geography violated the equal protection clause of the U.S. Constitution. Following the publication of that pathbreaking book, numerous court cases were filed, litigated, and challenged, and state and federal officials made frenzied efforts to "mandate" educational achievement. Ten years later, Wise wrote another book called *Legislated Learning: The Bureaucratization of the American Classroom,* in which he meticulously documented the "excessive rationalization" of educational decisionmaking. He predicted that the centralization and red tape created by these well-intended reforms would lead to a general decline in the quality of education.

In *For Better or For Worse? School Finance Reform in California,* Jon Sonstelie, Eric Brunner, and Kenneth Ardon take a careful look at the consequences of "legislated learning" in the nation's largest state. Not long after Wise formulated his equal protection arguments, *Serrano vs. Priest,* a class-action lawsuit filed in Los Angeles, challenged the constitutionality of California's school finance system. In 1971, the California Supreme Court agreed with the *Serrano* plaintiffs that children of "equal age, aptitude, motivation, and ability" did not have equal educational resources. The court ordered the state to bring the school finance system into compliance with the equal protection clause of the Fourteenth Amendment. Thirty years later, Sonstelie and his colleagues ask the question: Has school finance reform been good for Californians?

In the course of answering this question, the authors make several important points. First, they maintain that the reformers misunderstood the inequities under local school finance. Although many low-income and minority families lived in low-spending school districts, just as many lived in high-spending ones. As a result, reductions in revenue inequalities across districts did not help disadvantaged students as a whole. Second, the authors show that Proposition 13 affected school finance reform in ways that could not have been foreseen in 1971. By limiting property taxes, Proposition 13 eventually led to per pupil spending reductions. In the face of these reductions, school districts chose to hire fewer teachers, which resulted in a dramatic increase in the pupil-teacher ratio. Subsequent initiatives designed to restrict government spending also confounded or thwarted efforts to allot more resources to disadvantaged students. By the 1980s, the state was allocating revenues more equitably than before, but it did so more by "leveling down" high-spending districts than by raising low-spending ones.

One of the report's most compelling findings is also related to Proposition 13. Before 1978, the property taxes paid by commercial and industrial landowners subsidized school services for local residents. Proposition 13 effectively ended that subsidy by directing all property tax revenue to the state, which then reallocated school revenues according to a complex formula. As a result, school districts now benefit less from the largesse of commercial interests in local communities. The authors suggest that one policy option is to restore local finance in a way that is consistent with the *Serrano* ruling. This option, they maintain, would recapture some of the benefits of local control.

One of the benefits of local control may be higher student achievement. California's students were at or above national norms on standardized tests in the 1970s and 1980s but have fallen behind the rest of the country since that time. This poorer performance is not solely attributable to the recent influx of students with limited English proficiency. Even after controlling for such demographic changes in the student population, the authors find that California's students have lagged behind the rest of the nation on standardized tests. They conclude that the drop in test scores cannot necessarily be blamed on state finance but that the timing of the drop is suggestive.

This report is a companion piece to another PPIC report called *Equal Resources, Equal Outcomes? The Distribution of School Resources and Student Achievement in California,* by Julian R. Betts, Kim S. Rueben, and Anne Danenberg. By analyzing the distribution of teachers within districts, the authors found that the equalization of resources has not progressed as far as revenue allocations suggest. Taken together, these two reports highlight the complexity of an educational system that has been "legislated" and regulated for nearly 50 years. They also indicate

PPIC's commitment to meeting the challenge of improved K–12 education policy in California. It is our hope that in describing these complexities and their consequences, we will emphasize the most important goal of all—educating California's children for the 21st century.

David W. Lyon
President and CEO
Public Policy Institute of California

Summary

Thirty years ago, California embarked on a fundamental reform of its system for financing public schools. The impetus was *Serrano v. Priest,* a suit brought in 1968 by the Western Center on Law and Poverty. At the time, California school districts were raising more than half of their revenue by taxing local property. Districts set their own tax rates, subject to the approval of their voters. Because the property tax base differed dramatically across school districts, the *Serrano* plaintiffs maintained that the system was inequitable and thus in violation of the equal protection clause of the Fourteenth Amendment. The California Supreme Court agreed, touching off a series of legislative and popular initiatives. In 1978, Proposition 13 removed control of the property tax from school districts and assigned it to the state. In a very short time, California went from a system in which each district determined its own revenue to one in which the state decided every district's revenue. This transformation is now complete, and it is time to take stock. Has state control of school finance been good for California? This report answers that question by reviewing its main consequences.

State Financing Has Not Directed More Revenue to Poor Families

Financing a service at the state rather than the local level allows the government to redistribute resources to achieve policy goals. In the case of California's public schools, this ability was limited by the nature of the inequities under local finance. Local finance did not discriminate against poor families as such. Many poor families lived in districts with low revenue per pupil, but just as many lived in districts with high revenue per pupil. Although *Serrano* and subsequent decisions set the parameters for public school finance, the state had considerable leeway in distributing revenues across districts. In particular, the state was free to determine where and how much revenue would be allocated in the form of categorical aid to districts. The state has used this freedom conservatively. It reduced revenue inequalities among districts, but it did not direct significantly more revenue to districts with high concentrations of disadvantaged children. In this respect, state finance has not improved on local finance.

State Finance Led to a Decline in Average Spending per Pupil

Concerns about the fair distribution of revenue prompted school finance reform, but a more recent concern is the sheer amount of resources provided to California's schools. Between 1970 and 1997, spending per pupil in California fell more than 15 percent relative to spending in other states. In attempting to explain this decline, some observers have pointed to the growing disjunction between the racial and ethnic makeup of California's voters and its students. This report suggests another cause, one that is linked to the shift from local to state finance. The local system relied on the property tax, about half of which was levied on commercial, industrial, and agricultural property. In effect, taxes on this nonresidential property subsidized homeowners and renters. State finance ended that subsidy, thereby increasing the marginal cost of school spending to residents. We estimate that ending this subsidy should have lowered the demand for educational spending by 10 to 15 percent, which is the decline actually observed.

This decline in spending per pupil forced school districts to economize. Districts chose to hire fewer teachers, leading to a large increase in the pupil-teacher ratio. In 1970, California's pupil-teacher ratio was 8 percent above the average for other states; by 1997, it was 38 percent above that average. This increase was not accompanied by a fall in average teachers' salaries, another way in which districts might have economized. After investigating the question of teachers' salaries, we conclude that districts probably could not have reduced salaries without jeopardizing their ability to attract and retain competent teaching staffs.

California's high pupil-teacher ratio is often linked to the poor performance of California students on the National Assessment of Educational Progress. Another cause of that poor performance may be the relatively large percentage of California students whose native language is not English. Using data on the backgrounds of students, we examine how much of the poor performance of California students is due to these demographic differences. We find that these differences explain some, but not all, of the gap between California students and students in other states. We also examine data from earlier achievement tests, concluding that California students performed somewhat better before the conversion to state finance.

The Reactions of Parents Have Been Moderate

Families with school-age children have responded in two basic ways to the perceived decline in public school quality. Some have enrolled their children in private school, and some have donated time and money to their local schools. Both reactions have been strongest among high-income families. Among families in the top 10 percent of the income distribution, private school enrollments rose from 14 percent in 1970 to 21 percent in 1990. Among families in the next 10 percent of the income distribution, enrollments increased from 10 to 14 percent during the same period. There was no increase for families in the lower 60 percent of the income distribution. Likewise, voluntary contributions to public schools have been most significant in high-income communities. A few schools received contributions in excess of $500 per pupil, but more than 90 percent of the state's students attended a school in which such contributions came to less than $100 per pupil.

State Finance Has Not Equalized Educational Quality Across Districts

California's school finance reform focused on the distribution of revenues, but the ultimate goal of reformers was to equalize educational opportunities. If this goal had been achieved, residents would not continue to pay large premiums for houses in desirable school districts. We estimated these premiums for Los Angeles and Orange Counties and found a wide variety across school districts. These disparities indicate that parents perceive large differences in quality across school districts in those areas.

From the perspective of the original reformers, California's school finance reform must be judged a failure. It has not fundamentally realigned school revenues to the benefit of poor families, and it has not equalized the quality of school districts. Furthermore, it has equalized revenue by leveling down, decreasing average spending per pupil and increasing the state's pupil-teacher ratio relative to other states. Although state finance is not necessarily to blame for the poor performance of California's students on standardized achievement tests, it remains true that student achievement has not improved under state finance.

The Worst of Both Worlds?

In one sense, it may be premature to judge school finance reform. California has changed the way it finances its schools, but it has not changed the way it governs them. Voters still elect school boards to govern their schools, but these boards no longer have the power to tax. The state controls how funds are spent, but its only mechanism for governance is legislation—a blunt and often ineffective instrument. The lack of coordination between governance and financing poses a significant problem. As long as school finance is centralized, it may be helpful to centralize school governance as well. If local control is preferable, California should consider reintroducing a system of local finance consistent with the *Serrano* ruling.

One way to align state governance and finance is to eliminate school districts altogether. Such a system would replace legislative rulemaking with bureaucratic control, making it easier to allocate state resources according to need. This arrangement would also make it easier to hold teachers, principals, and schools accountable to state guidelines. Charter schools offer another way to implement state finance with less bureaucracy. Authorized in 1992, such schools operate according to their own goals and procedures and are exempt from most state regulations. Under a 1998 law, charter schools may receive block grants equal to what they would receive from a typical school district. As these schools proliferate, however, the state may come under increasing pressure to regulate them, again raising the question of whether public schools can be truly local without their own sources of revenue.

If the answer to that question is no, as the Legislative Analyst argues, and if local governance is desirable, then the state should consider giving school districts the authority to raise their own revenue. Our reading of the *Serrano* decision suggests that differences in revenue per pupil are tolerable if differences in property wealth are effectively neutralized. Equalizing district power, as originally proposed by the *Serrano* plaintiffs, satisfies that requirement. Under that plan, the same tax rate would produce the same revenue per pupil, regardless of the district's tax base. In effect, the state guarantees that every district has the same tax base. It does so by providing the difference between what the district would raise if its chosen tax rate were applied to the guaranteed base and what the district actually raises by applying that rate to its own base. This option, however, would require a constitutional provision to remove the 1 percent property tax limit imposed by Proposition 13.

Significant reform in either direction—toward state governance or local finance—will not be accomplished easily and is thus unlikely to occur. Insofar as this remains the case, school finance reform will have yielded neither the equity of a state-run system nor the flexibility and accountability of a decentralized one.

Contents

Figures

Tables

Acknowledgments

Throughout the preparation of this monograph, we benefited greatly from the help and advice of several people. Shandy Rieger, Kevin Shillito, Christiana Stoddard, Brian Duncan, and Dan Ryan provided excellent research assistance; Paul Goldfinger, John Mockler, and Fred Silva educated us about various aspects of California's school finance system; Lawrence Picus and Kim Rueben made valuable comments on an earlier draft of this monograph; and Peter Richardson worked closely with us to sharpen our prose. We are grateful to each of them.

We are particularly grateful to three people: Ray Reinhard, Paul Warren, and Bill Whiteneck. Each gave generously of his time in explaining the history and operation of California's school finance system, and each made extensive comments on an earlier draft. If we have managed to convey at least a portion of what we have learned from them, we will have accomplished something useful.

Finally, we wish to thank the staff of the Public Policy Institute of California who have helped in many ways, including providing a pleasant and stimulating environment for the preparation of this monograph.

The authors are solely responsible for this monograph's content.

1. Introduction

Over the last three decades, California has fundamentally
transformed its system of public school finance. In 1970, the system was
financed locally. School districts levied their own property tax rates,
subject to the approval of their voters. The state supplemented that
revenue with foundation aid, which it distributed according to a simple
formula. The state now controls 90 percent of school district revenue,
and the districts themselves have few options for raising their own
revenue. This transformation from local to state finance was caused by
two events. The first was the 1971 ruling of the California Supreme
Court in *Serrano v. Priest*. The court found that California's system of
local finance was unconstitutional, leaving the legislature the task of
designing a new system. The second event was the passage of
Proposition 13, which took control of the property tax from school
districts and gave it to the state. As with many such transformations, this
one happened incrementally and without a clear vision. It may be time

to consider its consequences. Has state control of school finance been good for California?

This important question lacks a simple answer, yet we believe that Californians should be asking it. We are not alone in this belief. Elizabeth Hill, the Legislative Analyst, has recently called for a *K–12 Master Plan* that would sort out the proper role of state and local government in the financing and governance of California's public schools.[1] This Master Plan is envisioned as "a forum to review the state's existing policies." We intend this monograph to contribute to that review.

We borrow liberally from three excellent studies of California's school finance reform. Elmore and McLaughlin (1982) provide a fascinating account of the origins of the *Serrano* suit and the response of the state legislature. Unfortunately, their account ends in 1982, just as the legislature was clarifying the final elements of that response.[2] Picus (1991b) provides a complete account of these events up through the early 1990s, and Rubinfeld (1995) relates those events to other changes to state and local finance during that period. The present study differs from its precursors by focusing on the consequences of reform. After reviewing the 1970 school finance system in Chapter 2 and the *Serrano* suit in Chapter 3, we explore the effects of that landmark decision on subsequent reforms. The court ruled that differences in property tax revenue per pupil across districts could not be related to differences in the property wealth of those districts. It also recognized the authority of

---

[1] Hill (1999).

[2] Carroll and Park (1983) also analyzed school finance reform in California, but their analysis covers the period before Proposition 13. As we describe in Chapter 3, Proposition 13 was the critical event in the transformation to state finance.

the legislature to determine the special needs of school districts, giving the state considerable latitude in allocating revenue among districts.

Chapter 4 examines how the state has used that latitude. Although state finance led to a more equal distribution of revenue across school districts, this equality was achieved more by leveling down high-spending districts than by leveling up low-spending ones. In Chapter 5, we argue that this outcome was a natural consequence of California's form of state finance, which raised the marginal cost of school spending to homeowners. This higher marginal cost, in turn, lowered the demand for such spending.

Chapter 6 examines how this decline in spending affected school districts. We find that the chief effect was larger class sizes. California school districts did not decrease the average salary of teachers, another way they might have absorbed the decline in revenue. This outcome does not imply that California districts were paying their teachers too much, however. Our findings indicate that the average salary of teachers in California kept pace with that of nonteachers in the state. In that respect, school districts were responding to market forces.

The first six chapters of the report show that state finance led to a more equitable distribution of revenue among districts and a decline in average resources as measured by the number of teachers per pupil. Chapter 7 explores the notion that this decline in resources may have caused a decline in student achievement. Although achievement tests in the 1970s and early 1980s indicate that California students were on a par with students in the rest of the country, California students have performed poorly on standardized exams in recent years. This downward trend in student achievement is confirmed by results from the Scholastic Aptitude Test and is only partly explained by demographic differences

3

between California and other states. Although it is difficult to establish a causal link between state finance and low test scores, it remains the case that student achievement has declined since the transition to state control of school finance.

Chapters 8 through 10 study the way families have responded to these developments. Chapter 8 examines private school enrollments, which have experienced a modest increase among high-income families in California. Chapter 9 tracks another response to declining school quality, voluntary contributions to public schools. Chapter 10 examines a third expression of the demand for good public schools: namely, the premiums some families are willing to pay to live in certain school districts. If state finance had equalized quality across school districts, these premiums should be small. Our study of Los Angeles and Orange Counties reveals a wide range of premiums, indicating persistent differences in district quality as perceived by parents.

Chapter 11 summarizes the evidence presented in Chapters 2 through 10 and returns to the question of whether state control of school finance has been good for California. We conclude that California schools have worsened under state finance, which is at least partly responsible for the decline. In one sense, however, state finance has not yet had a fair trial. California has changed the way it finances its schools, but it has not changed the way it governs them. One way to improve public education may be to align the institutions that govern schools with those that finance them. This alignment could be accomplished in either of two ways: by fully implementing state governance or by reintroducing a system of local finance that would satisfy the courts. After outlining several policy options, we conclude by noting the potential obstacles to either sort of reform.

2. Local Finance and the Origin of School Finance Reform

The impetus for California's school finance reform was *Serrano v. Priest.* The initial *Serrano* complaint was filed in 1968 and reached the California Supreme Court in 1971. The complaint focused on inequalities in revenue per pupil across school districts. This chapter describes the origins of the complaint and the school finance system that existed in California at the time. It also examines the sources of revenue inequalities and how revenue was related to the characteristics of students and their families.

Serrano v. Priest has its legal origins in the equal protection clause of the Fourteenth Amendment. Congress drafted the amendment immediately after the Civil War with the intent of protecting the rights of newly freed slaves.[1] The equal protection clause prohibited any state from enacting laws that would "deny to any person within its jurisdiction

---

[1] For a history of the Fourteenth Amendment, see Nelson (1988).

the equal protection of its laws." For the first 85 years after passage of the amendment, the Supreme Court applied it mainly to economic regulation. In *Yick Wo v. Hopkins (1886)*, the court invalidated a San Francisco ordinance that discriminated against Chinese laundries. In *Lochner v. New York (1905)*, it struck down a New York state law prohibiting bakers from working longer than ten hours a day.

Under Chief Justice Earl Warren, the court moved beyond economic regulation to overturn state laws in a host of other areas, an extension Kurland (1963) has dubbed "the egalitarian revolution." In *Brown v. Board of Education (1954)*, the court outlawed racial segregation in public schools. In *Griffin v. Illinois (1956)*, it invalidated a fee charged to criminal defendants for trial transcripts because the fee abridged the legal rights of the poor. In *Harper v. Virginia Board of Elections (1966)*, the court used a similar rationale to rule against Virginia's poll tax. In *Baker v. Carr (1962)*, the court overturned Tennessee's legislative districting because districts were not of equal populations. In each of these cases and in several others, the court relied on the equal protection clause to reach its conclusion. When it came to fundamental rights such as education, criminal trials, or voting, and where a state law appeared to discriminate among people in providing access to those rights, the court required a powerful rationale for the law, particularly when the discrimination occurred along racial or economic lines.

On the basis of those rulings, one can easily envision other extensions of the equal protection clause. Arthur Wise (1967) was the first to articulate the extension to public school finance. At that time, every state except Hawaii depended heavily on local property taxes to finance its schools. Because the property tax bases of school districts differed widely, this system produced large variations among districts in revenue per pupil. These variations could be ascribed to differences in wealth in that they were caused by variations in district tax bases. They could also be ascribed to geography because the tax base of a family's school district depended on where it lived. Wise argued that these variations were unconstitutional. After a detailed analysis of the Supreme Court's equal protection rulings, he advanced three "tentative arguments."[2]

> Discrimination in education on account of race is unconstitutional. Discrimination in criminal proceedings on account of poverty is unconstitutional. Therefore, discrimination in education on account of poverty is unconstitutional.

> Discrimination in education on account of race is unconstitutional. Discrimination in legislative apportionment on account of geography is unconstitutional. Therefore, discrimination in education on account of geography is unconstitutional.

> Discrimination in education on account of race is unconstitutional. Discrimination in voting on account of poverty is unconstitutional. Therefore, discrimination in education on account of poverty is unconstitutional.

As a result of any of these three arguments, he reasoned, the court could require equalization of revenue per pupil across school districts.

Wise's position is often characterized as "one scholar, one dollar," an analogy to the court's "one man, one vote" decision in *Baker v. Carr*.[3] That is not how he intended it to be read, however. In the Preface to *Rich Schools, Poor Schools: The Promise of Equal Educational Opportunity*, he cautioned against "simplistic" solutions. His ultimate concern was the quality of a child's education, and he recognized that equal quality might require more resources for students from disadvantaged backgrounds.

---

[2]Wise (1967), p. 167.

[3]Minorini and Sugarman (1999), p. 36.

At about the same time, similar arguments were being advanced by Harold Horowitz, a law professor at UCLA. Horowitz (1966) focused on two types of inequities within a public school district: the failure to provide the same services at schools in advantaged and disadvantaged areas and the failure "to provide compensatory educational programs for culturally deprived children."[4] Like Wise, Horowitz was ultimately focused on equality in educational opportunity rather than equality of resources as such. In a subsequent article, Horowitz and Neitring (1968) applied the same argument to inequalities among school districts.

The legal theorizing of Wise and Horowitz laid the intellectual groundwork for the *Serrano* complaint. As Enrich (1995) observed, another force was also at work. In the 1960s, the nation's political agenda began moving from civil rights to poverty. The civil rights movement had successfully attacked racial discrimination in many areas, yet many blacks continued to live in poverty. As it became evident that removing overt forms of discrimination left other problems unaddressed, the movement began to confront the problem of poverty itself. One manifestation of this new agenda was President Johnson's war on poverty, which, among other things, initiated the Office of Economic Opportunity.

The egalitarian revolution came together with the war on poverty at the Western Center of Law and Poverty. The center was a Los Angeles public interest law firm funded by the Office of Economic Opportunity.[5] It was headed by Derrick A. Bell, Jr., who had worked with Thurgood

---

[4]Horowitz (1966), p. 1148.

[5]Elmore and McLaughlin (1982) provide a detailed description of the origins of the *Serrano* complaint.

Marshall in the NAACP Legal Defense and Educational Fund.[6] Bell met Horowitz, and the two decided to initiate a suit challenging the constitutionality of California's school finance system. Reinhold (1972) described Horowitz as the "house intellectual" in this effort; the initial complaint "was thrashed out amid great piles of law books and statistics in Mr. Horowitz's cubicle at the UCLA Law School."

The complaint had three causes of action. The first was a class action suit on behalf of 27 school children in Los Angeles County and other unnamed school children throughout the state. The second cause of action was also a class action suit on behalf of the parents of these children. The first plaintiff listed was John Serrano, Jr., acting individually and on behalf of his eight-year-old son, John Anthony Serrano, who was attending an elementary school in the Whittier City School District. The defendants were a list of public officials in the state, headed by Ivy Baker Priest, the state treasurer. The third cause of action sought a court order requiring that the defendants reform California's school finance system.

The complaint was filed in Los Angeles Superior Court on August 23, 1968. Although the nature of the *Serrano* complaint was to change as events unfolded, the initial complaint reveals the underlying motive. In the first cause of action, the plaintiffs' lawyers focused on inequalities in educational opportunity across school districts. Although they pointed to evidence of inequalities in expenditures per pupil, they were quick to argue that equal expenditures per pupil would not be constitutional "where pupils have differing educational needs." They alleged that differences in the quality of education were systematically

---

[6]In 1969, Bell left the center to join the law faculty at Harvard.

9

related to race and wealth. In particular, the quality of education provided to a districts' children was alleged to be "a function of the wealth of the children's parents and neighbors, as measured by the tax base of the school district." Furthermore, the lawyers claimed that "a disproportionate number of school children who are black children, children with Spanish surnames, and children belonging to other minority groups reside in school districts in which a relatively inferior educational opportunity is provided." They also maintained that the quality of a child's education could be determined by a seemingly arbitrary event, a "geographical accident." As a result, children of "equal age, aptitude, motivation, and ability" did not have equal educational resources.

The second cause of action focused on inequities to taxpayers. In this case, the plaintiffs' lawyers alleged that taxpayers in some districts were required to pay higher tax rates than those in other districts to provide an equal or lesser educational opportunity for their children. In both the first and second causes, the lawyers maintained that California's school finance system violated the Fourteenth Amendment and "the fundamental law and Constitution of California." In the third cause, the plaintiffs sought a court order that would require that the defendants "re-allocate the funds available for financial support of the school system, including without limitation, funds derived from the taxation of real property."

Although the *Serrano* lawyers claimed that the school finance system violated the Fourteenth Amendment and the Constitution of California, they provided little evidence for their claims. The complaint included six tables of statistics showing disparities among districts in assessed value per pupil, tax rates, and revenue per pupil; none of these tables, however, linked educational resources to race, ethnicity, or wealth. This omission left basic questions unanswered. Was California's system of funding schools unfair to students and taxpayers? Did it in fact discriminate against poor, black, and Hispanic families?

School Districts

Answers to these questions require a detailed understanding of school districts and their funding. In 1970, California had 1,079 districts, enrolling a total of 4.8 million students. Sixty percent of those students were enrolled in the 236 unified school districts, districts with all grades from kindergarten through grade 12. The largest district, Los Angeles Unified, enrolled more than 650,000 students—more students than in each of the 25 smallest states. At the same time, half of the 723 elementary school districts had fewer than 364 students. Many of these smaller districts were in rural areas, but several were located in urban areas next to large unified districts. For the purposes of this report, we focus our attention on unified districts, relegating material on elementary and high school districts to Appendix A. However, the general patterns we discuss also apply to elementary and high school districts.

The Property Tax

Public school finance had evolved gradually in California until 1970.[7] From the early days of statehood, local school districts raised revenue by taxing the property in their jurisdictions. The tax was levied on the assessed value of property, which was based on market value. The assessor in each county established these values, and practices differed

---

[7]Picus (1991a) provides a brief history of California's school finance system.

among counties. In 1965, Assembly Bill 80 standardized the assessment process by requiring that assessors account for zoning classifications and fixing the ratio of assessed value to market value at 25 percent throughout the state.[8] The state also exempted portions of owner-occupied homes and business inventories from the property tax and compensated school districts for these exemptions through tax relief subventions. In 1969–70, the total assessed value of property in California was nearly $50 billion, 36 percent of which was accounted for by single family homes.[9] According to O'Sullivan, Sexton, and Sheffrin (1995), owner-occupied homes accounted for about 34 percent of total assessed value by the early 1990s. The balance came from other residential property (31 percent), commercial and industrial property (26 percent), and agricultural and vacant land (9 percent).

In 1970, school districts could levy two types of property tax rates on the assessed value of property within their boundaries.[10] The first was a "general purpose tax rate," which was subject to a maximum established by the state legislature. Districts could exceed the maximum only by a majority vote of their electorate. In these referendums, a district would propose a tax rate and a period of time for which the rate would apply. The period could be unlimited, and a district could propose a new tax rate even if its existing tax rate had not expired. If such a proposal failed, the existing rate continued. Conversely, if a new proposal failed and the existing tax rate had expired, the district's rate reverted to the statutory maximum. In 1968–69, all but 11 districts had tax rates exceeding their

---

[8]Doerr (February 1998), p. 9.

[9]Doerr (March 1998), p. 9.

[10]Our description of school finance in 1970 is from the Legislative Analyst (1971) and Barro (1971).

maximum, making frequent tax rate referendums a necessity.[11] Between 1966 and 1972, there were 1,216 of these referendums, 52 percent of which were successful.[12] Among unified districts, the general purpose tax rate ranged from 1 percent to 4.7 percent of assessed value, with an average of 3.1 percent. In terms of market values, those rates were equivalent to a range from 0.25 percent to 1.2 percent with an average of 0.8 percent. The state legislature also granted school districts the authority to levy a second type of tax rate, "permissive override taxes," which were taxes for particular purposes such as special education. These taxes did not require direct voter approval. By 1970, the legislature had authorized 43 permissive override taxes. The average tax among unified districts was 0.8 percent of assessed value and ranged from 0 percent to 1.9 percent.

School districts levied about 40 percent of the property taxes in California. In 1970, the sum of general purpose and permissive override tax rates averaged 3.9 percent of assessed value for unified districts. For property owners in an elementary and high school district, the total tax rate was similar in magnitude. The rate averaged 2.1 percent of assessed value for elementary school districts and 2.0 percent for high school districts, for a sum of 4.1 percent. In comparison, in 1969–70, the total property tax rate levied by all local governments averaged 9.92 percent of assessed value, which was equivalent to 2.48 percent of market value.[13]

A basic premise of the *Serrano* complaint was that assessed value per pupil was unequally distributed across California school districts. Figure 2.1 depicts the distribution of assessed value per pupil across unified

---

[11]Legislative Analyst (1971), Part V, p. 12.

[12]Alexander and Bass (1974), p. 51.

[13]Doerr (March 1998), p. 2.

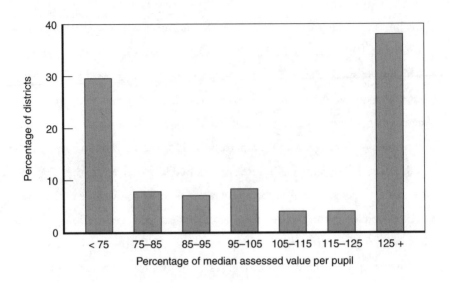

Figure 2.1—Distribution of Assessed Value per Pupil, by District:
Unified Districts in 1969–70

districts in 1969–70. As alleged in the *Serrano* complaint, assessed value per pupil did vary widely across school districts. To illustrate this variation, we have separated districts into seven categories based on their assessed value per pupil. The first category is districts with assessed value per pupil less than 75 percent of the median assessed value per pupil. As the figure shows, nearly 30 percent of districts fell in this category. Nearly 40 percent of districts fell in the last category, districts with assessed value per pupil greater than 125 percent of the median.

Table 2.1 lists the assessed value per pupil for the largest school districts, those with more than 50,000 students. These nine districts enrolled 26 percent of California's public school students. The disparities in assessed value resemble statewide patterns. For unified districts, the median assessed value per pupil was $12,243. Assessed value per pupil in San Francisco Unified was more than twice the

Table 2.1

Assessed Value per Pupil in 1969–70
in Districts with More Than 50,000
Students

District	Assessed Value[a] per Pupil ($)
Garden Grove	5,326
San Juan	6,235
Fresno	6,522
Sacramento	9,096
San Diego	9,630
Median	**12,243**
Los Angeles	13,455
Oakland	15,700
Long Beach	16,887
San Francisco	27,829

[a]25 percent of market value.

median, and assessed value per pupil in Garden Grove Unified was less than half of the median. Garden Grove, Fresno, San Juan, and Sacramento were less than 75 percent of the median, whereas Oakland, Long Beach, and San Francisco were more than 125 percent of the median.

State Aid

These disparities in assessed value were partly offset by state aid, which was inversely related to a district's assessed value per pupil. Figure 2.2 summarizes this relationship for elementary school students in 1970. (A similar formula covered high school students.) The state supplied both supplemental and equalization aid. In the hypothetical case of a district with no assessed value, the district would receive equalization aid of $355 per pupil and supplemental aid of $125 per pupil. A $100

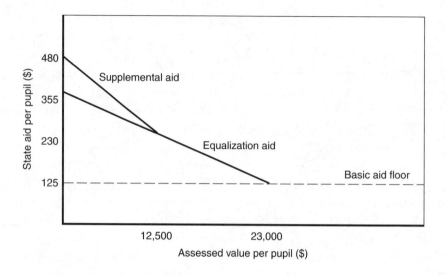

Figure 2.2—Foundation Aid for Elementary School Students

increase in assessed value would lower both equalization and
supplemental aid by $1 for a total reduction of $2. This rate of decrease
would continue until supplemental aid fell to $0 at an assessed value of
$12,500, at which point total state aid would equal $230. Further
increases in value would decrease equalization aid at the same rate of $1
of aid for $100 of assessed value until assessed value per pupil reached
$23,000, at which point the district would receive $125 per pupil. This
level was a floor on state aid to a district, which was referred to as basic
aid. Further increases in assessed value per pupil beyond $23,000 did
not decrease state aid below this floor.

Equalization and supplemental aid were a foundation program that
many states used at the time. Under the typical program, the state
provided each school district with enough revenue to attain a basic level
of spending, which was referred to as the foundation level. Each district
was responsible for a share of the foundation level—a share determined

16

by applying a state-specified tax rate to the district's assessed value. The state then contributed the difference between the foundation level and the local share.

For California's equalization aid, the foundation level in 1969–70 was $355 per elementary and $488 per high school student. These foundation levels were considerably lower than the revenue districts actually raised. In 1969–70, total revenue per pupil was $728 for elementary school districts, $952 for high school districts, and $817 for unified districts. The state-specified tax rates used to compute local contributions were also much lower than the actual rates that school districts levied. For elementary school students, this "computational tax rate" was 1 percent, in contrast to the average for elementary school districts of 2.1 percent. For high school students, the computational tax rate was 0.8 percent, and the average rate was 2.0 percent. In fact, the average property tax revenue raised by both elementary and high school districts was greater than the foundation levels for each. However, many districts exceeding the foundation level still received equalization aid because their local contribution was determined by the computational tax rate, not their actual tax rate.

Supplemental aid was the second foundation program. For elementary school students, the foundation level for supplemental aid was $125 per pupil and the computational tax rate was 1 percent. With an assessed value per pupil of $12,500, a district's local contribution would equal the foundation level, and thus the state's contribution would be $0. This cutoff level was slightly above the median assessed value per pupil, so supplemental aid went only to districts with relatively low assessed value. For high school students, the foundation level for supplemental aid was even lower—$72 per pupil.

Under a standard foundation program, districts with very high assessed value per pupil might receive no state aid. California deviated from this standard program because of its basic aid floor, which was a holdover from the original state aid program—a flat grant of $125 per pupil.[14] When the state legislature adopted the foundation program in 1947, it retained this grant as a minimum in the foundation aid formula. Under the formula, an increase in assessed value per pupil decreased a district's equalization aid until that aid fell to $125 per pupil. For elementary students, this occurred at an assessed value of $23,000 per pupil, which was midway between the 75th and 95th percentiles for unified districts. Beyond this point, further increases in assessed value did not cause a decline in state aid. All districts received at least $125 per pupil, regardless of their property wealth.

There were other minor modifications and exceptions to this basic formula. For small districts, equalization aid increased with enrollment in discrete steps. For example, a district with 76 students received the same aid as a district with 100 students, based on the notion that the two should employ the same number of teachers. Aside from this detail, small districts received essentially the same aid as large districts. If a district had the maximum enrollment for its step, it would receive the same aid per pupil as a large district with the same assessed value per pupil. The foundation program also contained a bonus of $20 per pupil for districts that had recently unified and a bonus of $30 per student in grades 1 through 3 for districts whose class sizes in those grades did not exceed a specified maximum.

---

[14]The Constitution required that the state provide districts a grant of $120 per student. The grant was increased to $125 by a statute passed in 1957. See Legislative Analyst (1971), Part III, p. 1.

The state distributed $1.2 billion to districts through this program in 1969–70. In addition, it distributed about $165 million for four other programs.[15] More than half of this sum went to special education programs. About $40 million of state funds was spent on programs to enhance the educational achievement of children from poor families. The state distributed these funds case by case after reviewing applications from school districts. There was also a program for gifted students, which received about $8 million in 1969–70.

Figure 2.3 summarizes the revenue sources for unified districts during this time. Property taxes include the homestead and business inventory tax relief subventions provided by the state. This source accounted for 58 percent of the total revenue of unified districts. The second largest source was state aid, constituting 34 percent of the total. Federal aid and other local revenue were minor sources.

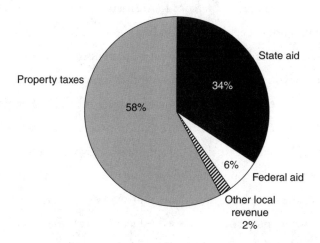

Figure 2.3—Sources of District Revenues: Unified Districts in 1969–70

---

[15]State of California (1971), p. 51.

The Distribution of Total Revenue Across School Districts

A foundation program offsets inequities in the distribution of assessed value because it allocates more state aid to districts with lower assessed value per pupil. Its effect on the distribution of revenue, however, depends on the property tax rates school districts actually levy. For a foundation program to achieve equality across school districts, two conditions are sufficient. The first is that all school districts levy a tax rate equal to the state's computational tax rate. The second is that the foundation level exceed the revenue per pupil raised by each district. In that case, each district would receive some state aid, and all districts would have total revenue per pupil equal to the foundation level. Districts with low assessed values would receive just enough state aid to offset the higher property tax revenue of wealthier districts.

Because there are myriad reasons for districts to levy different tax rates, we would not expect the first condition to obtain. The most obvious sources of variation in tax rates are differences in the preferences and incomes of voters in each district. Another important but less widely recognized source of variation is the marginal price of school spending, which in this case is determined by the share of property that is nonresidential. To illustrate this concept, imagine two districts with the same assessed value per pupil, and suppose that the residents of the two districts have the same tastes and incomes. The only difference between the districts is the source of the assessed value. Whereas the first district is made up entirely of owner-occupied housing, industrial property makes up half of the second district's assessed value. If both districts choose the same tax rate, they raise the same amount of revenue per pupil. In the district with industrial property, however, homeowners pay only half of the the overall tax burden; industrial property owners pay the other half. In general, the larger the share of nonresidential property in a district, the less residents must pay to raise each dollar in revenue. Because voters in the all-residential district would face a larger tax bill for any given tax rate, they would be more likely to choose a lower tax rate.

Although artificial, this example illustrates a basic point. In comparing two school districts, variations in assessed value may have very different effects on spending per pupil. If one district has higher assessed value than another because it contains commercial or industrial property, we would expect it to spend more on its schools. If the difference in assessed value is strictly due to differences in residential property, however, the district is more likely to assess a lower rate than to spend more on its schools. In Chapter 5, we attempt to sort out these different effects in a systematic way. We also examine the role of income and preferences in affecting school spending. At this point, we merely raise these issues to provide background for interpreting the relationship between assessed value per pupil and tax rates across California school districts.

Figure 2.4 plots the tax rates of unified districts against their assessed value per pupil. The relationship between the two variables is clearly negative. Districts with higher assessed values per pupil tended to have lower tax rates; even so, they may have raised more property tax revenue. To address this question, Figure 2.4 includes a curve representing combinations of tax rates and assessed value per pupil that would yield $478 per pupil—the average property tax revenue per pupil for unified districts.

As the figure demonstrates, most districts with high assessed value per pupil lie above this curve, indicating that they had more than average

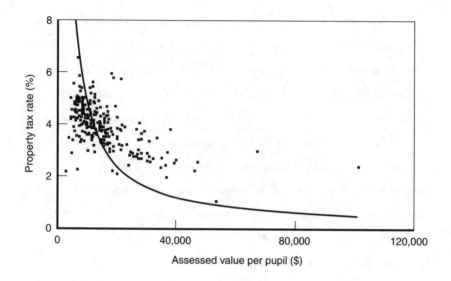

Figure 2.4—Property Tax Rates Compared with Assessed Value per Pupil:
Unified Districts in 1969–70

property tax revenue per pupil. The strong positive relationship between assessed value and property tax revenue is depicted even more clearly in Figure 2.5. As the *Serrano* plaintiffs alleged, districts with high tax bases had lower property tax rates and higher property tax revenue per pupil.

In theory, differences in property tax revenue would have been offset by state aid. Figure 2.6 shows that districts with higher property tax revenue per pupil did tend to have lower state aid per pupil.

But as Figure 2.7 indicates, the net effect of property tax revenue and state aid shows that state aid only partially compensated for differences in assessed value per pupil. Districts with lower assessed value received more state aid, but this aid was not enough to offset their lower property tax revenue.

Table 2.2 illustrates this same point for the largest districts. As assessed value per pupil increases, property tax revenue per pupil also

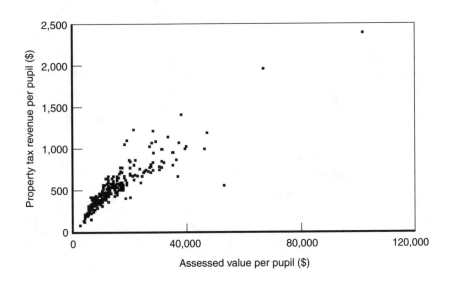

Figure 2.5—Property Tax Revenue per Pupil Compared with Assessed Value per Pupil: Unified Districts in 1969–70

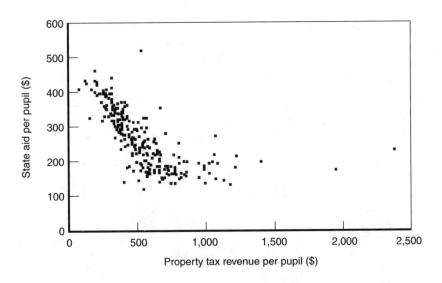

Figure 2.6—State Aid per Pupil Compared with Property Tax Revenue per Pupil: Unified Districts in 1969–70

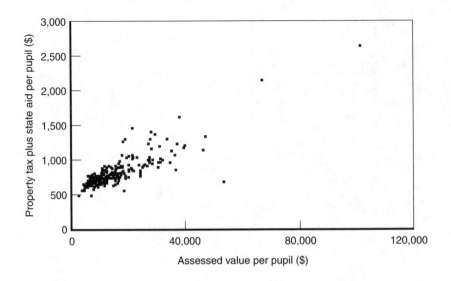

Figure 2.7—Property Tax Revenue and State Aid per Pupil Compared with
Assessed Value per Pupil: Unified Districts in 1969–70

Table 2.2

Revenue per Pupil in 1969–70 in Districts with More Than
50,000 Students
(in dollars)

District	Assessed Value[a] per Pupil	Property Taxes	State Aid	Property Taxes Plus State Aid
Garden Grove	5,326	224	391	615
San Juan	6,235	308	377	685
Fresno	6,522	323	332	655
Sacramento	9,096	385	298	683
San Diego	9,630	431	289	720
Los Angeles	13,455	538	240	778
Oakland	15,700	645	228	873
Long Beach	16,887	598	189	787
San Francisco	27,829	1,063	218	1,281

[a]25 percent of market value.

24

increases. Even though state aid per pupil drops, the sum of property tax revenue and state aid per pupil also increases. For example, San Francisco's assessed value per pupil was more than five times that of Garden Grove, and its property tax revenue per pupil was nearly five times as high. Although San Francisco's state aid per pupil was only 56 percent of Garden Grove's, this difference was not nearly enough to offset the differences in property tax revenue. The sum of property tax revenue and state aid per pupil was twice as high for San Francisco as for Garden Grove.

Figure 2.8 illustrates the net effect of property tax revenue and state aid for all unified districts in 1969–70. The figure shows the distribution of total revenue per pupil—the sum of property taxes, state aid, federal aid, and other local revenue. A comparison of Figure 2.8 with Figure 2.1 reveals an important point. Total revenue per pupil did vary significantly

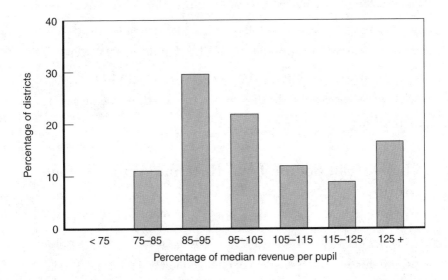

Figure 2.8—Distribution of Total Revenue per Pupil, by District: Unified Districts in 1969–70

across districts, but the variation was not nearly as great as it was for assessed value per pupil. As in Figure 2.1, Figure 2.8 classifies districts into seven categories. In Figure 2.8, the classification depends on the relationship of a district's total revenue per pupil to the median of total revenue per pupil for all unified districts. Although Figure 2.1 showed that nearly 30 percent of districts had assessed value per pupil less than 75 percent of the median assessed value per pupil, Figure 2.8 shows that no district had total revenue per pupil less than 75 percent of the median. Similarly, nearly 40 percent of all districts had assessed value per pupil greater than 125 percent of the median, but less than 20 percent had total revenue per pupil greater than 125 percent of the median.

The distribution of revenue per pupil in Figure 2.8 is somewhat misleading because some of the highest revenue districts in 1969–70 were also quite small. By weighting districts according to enrollment, Figure 2.9 more accurately depicts the distribution of revenue per pupil. In terms of total revenue per pupil, only 25 percent of the districts fell between 95 and 105 percent of the median, but nearly 40 percent of the state's students were enrolled in those districts. Thus, when districts are weighted by enrollment, the distribution of revenue per pupil is more concentrated.

The Distribution of Total Revenue Across Income Groups

Figures 2.1 through 2.9 substantiate one of the underlying premises of the *Serrano* complaint. Districts with lower assessed value per pupil had two disadvantages: higher tax rates and lower revenue per pupil. A second premise of the *Serrano* complaint concerned the students in these districts. The complaint alleged that districts with lower assessed value

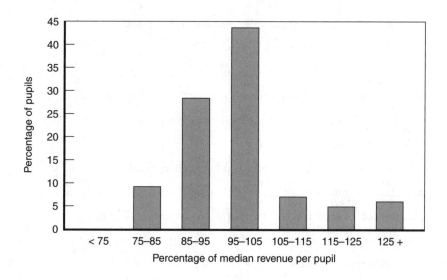

Figure 2.9—Distribution of Total Revenue per Pupil, by Pupils: Unified Districts in 1969–70

per pupil tended to have higher concentrations of poor and minority students, implying that California's school finance system discriminated against such students.

To investigate the link between family income and assessed value, we turn to data from the 1970 Census, which for the first time reported standard Census variables by school district. Although the Census reported statistics for only 739 of the 1,079 districts existing in 1969–70, those districts enrolled 98 percent of public school students in California. For these districts, we separated families into three categories based on their income. One category is families with annual incomes less than $7,000, which constituted 26 percent of all families. The second category is families with annual incomes greater than $15,000; these high-income families constituted 27 percent of all families. We refer to the remaining 47 percent of families as middle-income families.

Figure 2.10 shows the similar distribution of assessed value per pupil for each of these three groups. Between 20 and 30 percent of families in each group lived in a district with assessed value per pupil less than 75 percent of the median. Likewise, between 20 and 30 percent of each group lived in a district with assessed value per pupil greater than 125 percent of the median.

Because of the close relationship between assessed value per pupil and total revenue per pupil, the same general pattern should hold for the distribution of total revenue per pupil. As Figure 2.11 indicates, that distribution is also very similar for the three different income groups, indicating that California's school finance system did not discriminate against poor families as such.

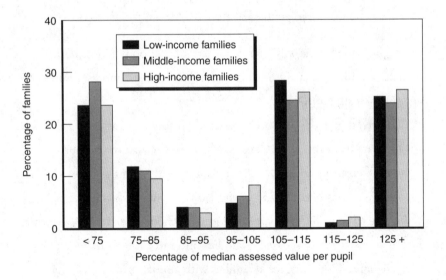

Figure 2.10—Distribution of Assessed Value per Pupil, by Family Income: Unified Districts in 1969–70

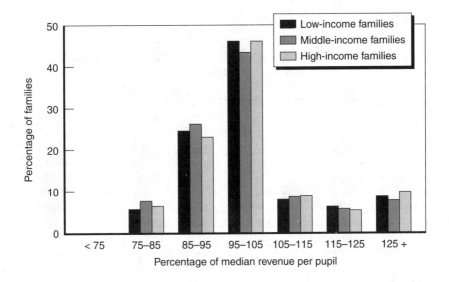

Figure 2.11—Distribution of Total Revenue per Pupil, by Family Income:
Unified Districts in 1969–70

The Distribution of Total Revenue, by Race and Ethnicity

The *Serrano* lawyers also alleged that California's system discriminated against minorities, specifically black and Hispanic students. To examine that claim, we combined data on the race and ethnicity of students in each district with data on assessed value for districts. The data on race and ethnicity come from the California State Testing Program. Figure 2.12 shows the distribution of assessed value per pupil for each of three groups: black pupils, Hispanic pupils, and other pupils. In general, black pupils attended districts with higher assessed value per pupil than other pupils, and Hispanic pupils attended districts with lower assessed value per pupil. The differences are not dramatic, however.

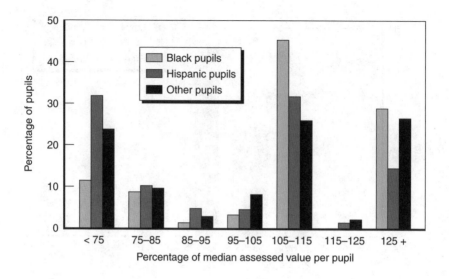

Figure 2.12—Distribution of Assessed Value per Pupil, by Race and Ethnicity: Unified Districts in 1969–70

Figure 2.13 shows the distribution of revenue per pupil for each of these three groups. Again, the distributions are very similar, indicating that California's finance system did not discriminate against minority students.

We have addressed the issue of discrimination the way the *Serrano* plaintiffs posed it. We have focused on differences in resources across school districts and found little evidence of discrimination along economic, racial, or ethnic lines. It is important to note, however, that there is another dimension along which this issue could be pursued: variations in resources among schools within a district. There could be little discrimination across school districts, yet considerable discrimination within districts.

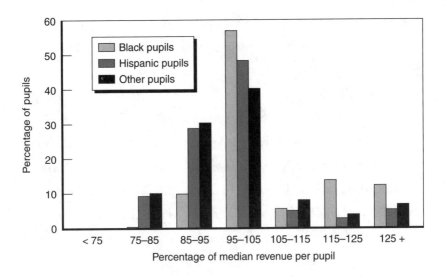

Figure 2.13—Distribution of Revenue per Pupil, by Race and Ethnicity:
Unified Districts in 1969–70

Conclusion

In 1970, California school districts had substantial autonomy. They
had their own tax bases and set their own tax rates. This autonomy
resulted in considerable inequality in revenue per pupil, the chief cause of
which was the wide variation in the tax bases of districts. Through its
foundation program, the state offset some of these differences. Districts
with low assessed value received more state aid than districts with high
assessed value, yet large differences in revenue per pupil remained.

Contrary to the claims of the *Serrano* plaintiffs, these inequalities did
not appear to be systematically related to race, ethnicity, or family
income. The distribution of revenue per pupil was approximately the
same for families in different income groups. Black students tended to
be enrolled in higher-revenue districts than other students, and Hispanic

students tended to be in lower-revenue districts. As in the case of income, however, there was more inequality within racial or ethnic groups than across those groups.

In reviewing California's system, we have focused on how revenue per pupil was distributed across different income, racial, and ethnic groups, and we have ignored any differences in the educational needs of those groups. In that respect, we have not done justice to the concerns originally expressed by Wise and Horowitz. That does not mean that we take these concerns lightly. We would take educational needs into account if we could devise an objective method to measure those needs. As we shall see, the courts have wrestled with the same problem.

3. From Local to State Finance

California's system of school finance evolved gradually over the first 120 years of statehood but was radically transformed over the next 20. In 1971, the *Serrano* case reached the California Supreme Court, which found California's school finance system to be unconstitutional and handed the legislature the task of redesigning it. Seven years later, the voters of California passed Proposition 13, which helped shape the new system. Less dramatic, but no less important, were the actions of the state legislature, whose task it was to absorb these twin shocks and to translate them into workable policies. This chapter describes these events and how they transformed the state's school finance system.

The First *Serrano* Ruling

The *Serrano* complaint was not initially tried in Superior Court. The defendants demurred, choosing not to challenge the plaintiffs' description of California's school finance system. Instead, they contended that the system would be constitutional even if the description were accurate. The trial judge agreed and dismissed the case. The *Serrano* lawyers appealed.

At about the same time, a similar suit was being tried in Illinois. In that case, *McInnis v. Shapiro,* the plaintiffs were the students in the Chicago Public School System and the defendant was the State of Illinois. The attorneys for the plaintiffs argued that Illinois's school finance system did not provide enough resources to meet the exceptional educational needs of Chicago's students, many of whom were from disadvantaged backgrounds. The suit was filed in federal court, and the court rejected the plaintiffs' argument, in part because educational need was too nebulous to provide a sound legal standard. The ruling was appealed to the U.S. Supreme Court, which affirmed the decision of the lower court without explaining its rationale.

The *McInnis* decision determined the fate of the *Serrano* appeal. In its decision, the Court of Appeals concluded that the *McInnis* and *Serrano* cases were essentially the same and that the *McInnis* decision therefore held for *Serrano* as well. The *Serrano* lawyers appealed to the California Supreme Court, narrowing their argument in response to the *McInnis* decision. They de-emphasized the arguments in their complaint's first cause of action, which focused on equality of educational opportunity and differing needs of school children, and stressed the arguments in their second cause of action, which focused on taxpayer equity.

This refocusing was aided by a new legal theory developed by John Coons, William Clune, and Stephen Sugarman in their 1970 book, *Private Wealth and Public Education.* In that book, the authors outlined a more conservative constitutional case against local school finance than the one advanced by Wise and Horowitz. They offered a definition of educational quality that is easy to quantify—"Quality is the sum of district expenditures per pupil; quality is money."[1] In that respect, they embraced the "simplistic" standard against which Wise had cautioned. This standard implied that the state had no obligation to address the exceptional needs of disadvantaged students, an implication Coons, Clune, and Sugarman readily acknowledged. "Discrimination by the state is our sole object; this excludes the duty to ameliorate cultural or natural disadvantages."[2] Their definition of quality did not entail equal expenditures per pupil in every district, however. According to their theory, it was perfectly permissible for one district to raise more revenue per pupil than another if it chose to levy a higher tax rate. It was not permissible, however, for one district to raise more revenue per pupil than another if both levied the same tax rate. That is, it was not permissible for revenue per pupil to depend on taxable wealth per pupil. They distilled their notion of school finance equity into "a simple formula with modest aspirations." "The quality of public education may not be a function of wealth other than the wealth of the state as a whole."[3] This principle subsequently became known as fiscal neutrality.

As a legal theory, fiscal neutrality was brilliant. It espoused a principle of justice that could be adjudicated easily. It did not require that the courts make the difficult judgments about educational quality demanded by the *McInnis* plaintiffs, nor did it require that the state adopt any particular school finance system. It did not turn the courts into a legislature, as the theories of Wise and Horowitz might have. In fact, Coons, Clune, and Sugarman went to great lengths to demonstrate

---

[1]Coons, Clune, and Sugarman (1970), p. 25.

[2]Coons, Clune, and Sugarman (1970), p. 9.

[3]Coons, Clune, and Sugarman (1970), p. 2.

that there were many possible systems that would be fiscally neutral, including the voucher. As we will describe below, they also proposed a state aid formula that would preserve local finance without violating fiscal neutrality.

In their appeal to the California Supreme Court, the *Serrano* lawyers stuck closely to the argument laid out by Coons, Clune, and Sugarman. The court accepted this argument in its entirety. In writing its opinion, the court employed the legal framework developed from the equal protection rulings of the U.S. Supreme Court. According to that framework, laws may distinguish among individuals if they pass one of two tests. For laws regulating economic activity, a state may classify and distinguish among individuals as long as those classifications bear some rational relationship to a legitimate state purpose. However, if the method in which the state classifies people is particularly suspect, as in the case of race, or if the activity the state regulates involves a fundamental right, as in the case of voting, the state's laws must withstand a heavier burden of proof called strict scrutiny. Under strict scrutiny, the state must show that it has a compelling interest for establishing the law and that the law is necessary to achieve that interest. In its 1971 *Serrano* decision, the California Supreme Court ruled that public education was a fundamental right and that school district wealth was a suspect classification. This was essentially the argument Wise had articulated in 1967.

Having identified both a fundamental right and a suspect classification, the court applied the standard of strict scrutiny. Was California's school finance system necessary to achieve a compelling state interest? The defendants argued that the compelling state interest was stated in the Education Code: "to strengthen and encourage local responsibility for control of public education." The court found that the current system was not necessary to achieve that interest. In fact, it declared that local control was "a cruel illusion for the poor school districts."[4] California's system did not withstand strict scrutiny and would not be constitutional if the facts maintained by the plaintiffs could be established.

In their initial complaint, the *Serrano* lawyers had claimed that California's system discriminated against poor families. In their petition for a hearing in the Supreme Court, they repeated that claim, stating that "a child attending California schools is afforded an educational opportunity that ranges from excellent to inadequate depending on the wealth of his parents and neighborhood."[5] They clarified this statement in the following footnote:

> While this correlation is not exact owing to occasional instances where the school population is drawn from poor families residing in a district which is composed largely of commercial property, petitioners alleged and could prove, if given the opportunity, that the relative wealth of school district residents correlates to a high degree with the relative wealth of school districts as measured by the assessed valuation per pupil.[6]

If the *Serrano* lawyers had been given the opportunity they requested, they would have been hard pressed to prove their allegation. They were never provided this opportunity, however, because the court dismissed the relationship between individual and district wealth as irrelevant.

---

[4]*Serrano v. Priest,* 5 Cal. 3d 584; 487 P.2d 1241; 96 Cal. Rptr. 601; hereafter *Serrano I.*

[5]Binder et al. (1970), p. 2.

[6]Binder et al. (1970), p. 3.

More basically, however, we reject defendants' underlying thesis that classification by wealth is constitutional so long as the wealth is that of the district, not the individual. We think that discrimination on the basis of district wealth is equally invalid.[7]

The court's ruling in this matter nicely illustrates the difference between legal theory and public policy. In reaching this conclusion, the court followed the logic of fiscal neutrality. If it had been thinking about public policy, however, it would have asked who might gain and who might lose from moving to a fiscally neutral system.

In 1974, three years after the Supreme Court ruling, a clearer picture of the distribution of revenue began to emerge.[8] John Mockler, then a consultant to the Assembly Ways and Means Committee, combined data on families receiving Aid to Families with Dependent Children (AFDC) with data on the assessed valuation of school districts. He found that 61 percent of California children covered by AFDC lived in districts above the average in assessed valuation per pupil. The second source of evidence was provided by Ronald Cox of the Senate Office of Research. For the first time, the Department of Health, Education, and Welfare had assembled 1970 Census data by school district. Cox analyzed these data and reported findings similar to those discussed in Chapter 2.

The *Serrano* lawyers were taken aback by these findings. Harold Horowitz conceded that the lawyers falsely assumed that "low income kids live in low wealth districts."[9] John McDermott, another attorney for the plaintiffs, agreed there was "probably an assumption on the part of everyone that this was true."[10] In commenting on the new evidence,

---

[7] *Serrano I.*
[8] See McCurdy (1974).
[9] McCurdy (1974).
[10] McCurdy (1974).

he said, "I'm not sure what I wrought." Charles Benson, a professor of education at University of California, Berkeley, and an expert in school finance who had advised the *Serrano* lawyers, explained the basis of this false assumption.

> People writing about the educational finance problem in the 1960's looked at Willowbrook (in Compton) and so on as against districts like Santa Monica, and they made the assumption there was a correlation between assessed valuation and household income. It was an eyeballing thing.[11]

The findings of Mockler and Cox were less disconcerting to Stephen Sugarman.

> What we really wanted to do was make the system rational. Then we can try to target additional moneys for specific needs (of poor children).

Whereas McDermott was unsure of what he had wrought, Sugarman understood and approved. The courts could invalidate the existing system but could not create a new system. That task fell to the legislature.

Senate Bill 90

The state legislature took up the task immediately. In 1972, it passed Senate Bill 90, which contained an important element of the new system. The bill actually served two goals: compliance with the *Serrano* decision and relief from the property tax. Property tax relief, which was supported by farm and business interests in the state, was one of Governor Reagan's top priorities.[12] That relief also aided compliance with *Serrano* because the case against the existing system was rooted in the uneven distribution of the property tax base. Reducing the role of

---

[11]McCurdy (1974).

[12]Kirst (1978) describes the coalitions supporting SB 90.

the property tax in that system would also weaken the constitutional case against it.

One option for reducing the role of the property tax was to increase state aid to schools, thereby shifting some of the burden of school finance from local to state revenue sources. SB 90 incorporated that option by increasing the foundation level in the state aid formula. For elementary students, the foundation level was increased from $355 to $765. For high school students, the increase was from $488 to $950. The effect of these increases was moderated by other changes. SB 90 increased the computational tax rate from 1 percent to 2.23 percent for elementary students and from 0.8 percent to 1.64 percent for high school students, thereby increasing the percentage of the foundation level provided by school districts. It also eliminated the unification bonus, the class size reduction bonus, and the supplemental aid program.

The net effect of these changes is depicted in Figure 3.1. The figure shows the relationship between assessed value per pupil and state aid per pupil both before and after SB 90. (The figure shows the formula for elementary students, although a similar picture applies for high school students.) Befitting the goal of *Serrano* compliance, low-wealth districts received the largest increases in state aid. A district with assessed value per pupil of $5,351, the 25th percentile in 1969–70, would have received $378 per pupil under the old formula and $645 per pupil under the new formula, an increase of $267. In comparison, total revenue per pupil in the 25th percentile was $645 per pupil. Districts with high assessed value received very small increases. A district with assessed value per pupil of $28,375, the 95th percentile in 1969–70, would have

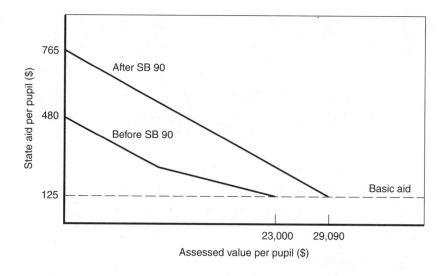

Figure 3.1—Foundation Aid for Elementary Students Under SB 90

received basic aid of $125 per pupil under the old formula and $133 per pupil under the new formula, an increase of $8.

With this increase in state aid, low-wealth districts had a choice: They could increase school spending or they could reduce property taxes. Because the increase in state aid did not change the marginal price of school spending faced by taxpayers, we would expect it to have little effect on their demand for school spending. In theory, the increase in state aid would be mostly spent on property tax relief. However, several studies investigating the effect of state aid on local government spending have reached a different conclusion.[13] An increase in lump-sum state aid tends to increase local government spending more than predicted by the theory. If California school districts were to follow this pattern, some of

––––––––––––––––––

[13]For an interpretation of this evidence and references to the literature, see Turnbull (1998).

the increased state aid would result in property tax relief and some would result in increased spending. In its analysis of SB 90, the Legislative Analyst[14] estimated that the increase in the foundation program would cost the state an additional $500 million per year, a considerable increase over the $1.1 billion the state spent on the foundation program in 1969–70. It also estimated that this increase would be split evenly between spending increases and property tax decreases.

SB 90 had other elements of property tax relief. It increased the homeowners exemption from $750 of assessed value to $1,750 of assessed value and increased the property tax exemption for business inventories from 30 percent to 50 percent of assessed value. The Legislative Analyst estimated that the new foundation formula and the expanded exemptions would cost nearly $1 billion a year. To offset these costs, SB 90 increased the sales tax rate from 3.75 percent to 4.75 percent and the bank and corporation tax rate from 7.6 percent to 9 percent. The net effect of these changes was to shift a significant share of revenues from local to state sources.

From today's perspective, however, this shift in revenue sources was less significant than the introduction of revenue limits. Each school district was assigned a limit on the sum of its property taxes and noncategorical state aid. The limits were based on the district's revenue per pupil from these sources in 1972–73 and then increased annually from that base. Revenue limits determined tax rate limits. The difference between a district's revenue limit and its state aid was the limit on its property tax revenue. Using the district's assessed value, the limit on revenue was translated into a limit on the tax rate. Under this system,

---

[14]Legislative Analyst (1972).

a district experiencing an increase in assessed value could be required to reduce its property tax rate. The tax rate limit was a limit on the district's total tax rate, which was the sum of its general purpose rate and its permissive override rates.

The annual growth rate of a district's revenue limit was determined by its current limit. Districts with lower limits were permitted higher growth rates. If its limit was below the foundation level, the growth rate was 15 percent. If it was above the foundation level but below a specified amount ($900 for elementary school districts), its revenue limit was increased by $65 per pupil. Above those amounts, the increase was a fraction of $65, a fraction inversely proportional to its current limit.[15] Figure 3.2 depicts the growth rate in revenue limits for elementary school

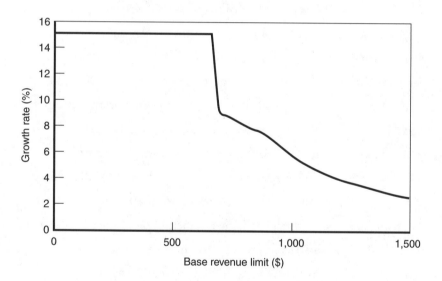

Figure 3.2—Growth Rate in Revenue Limits: Elementary School Districts

---

[15]These parameters were changed slightly by Assembly Bill 1267, which passed in 1973 as a trailer bill to SB 90.

districts. The lowest-spending districts were permitted growth rates of 15 percent, and the highest-spending districts were held to less than 3 percent. The difference in growth rates would cause revenue limits to converge over time. In conjunction with the new foundation formula, the convergence in revenue limits would also cause a convergence in revenue per pupil, as the spending in low-wealth districts was lifted by the increase in state aid and spending in high-wealth districts was constrained by the limits.

Limits on high-spending districts were a difficult political proposition, however. As Chapter 2 demonstrated, many of the large urban districts—including Los Angeles, Long Beach, Oakland, and San Francisco—were high-wealth, high-spending districts. San Francisco Unified was particularly exceptional, with assessed value and revenue per pupil in the 95th percentile for unified districts. Not only were these large districts wealthy, they were represented by many powerful legislators, several of whom held important positions in the Assembly and Senate. To gain the support of these legislators, Governor Reagan included in SB 90 a special categorical program called Education for Disadvantaged Youth (EDY).[16] The program had a budget of $82 million—a 50 percent increase in categorical aid over 1969–70. The funds were allocated according to a complicated formula that favored large urban districts, which had large numbers of disadvantaged students. In 1973–74, 396 districts received funds under this program with appropriations to districts ranging from $216 to $25 million.[17] SB 90 also included $25 million for another categorical program, the Early

---

[16]This political compromise is described in detail in Kirst (1978) and Elmore and McLaughlin (1982).

[17]California State Department of Education (1976).

Childhood Education Program, advocated by the State Superintendent of Public Instruction, Wilson Riles.

While EDY made revenue limits more palatable to the wealthy urban districts, all districts received relief from another provision of SB 90. Districts could override their revenue limits by a majority vote of their electorate. These referendums worked much like the tax rate referendums under the old system. The district would propose a certain dollar increment in its limit and a period of time for which the increase would be in place. If the proposal passed, the increment would be added each year to the revenue limit calculated according to the SB 90 formula. In 1973–74, 89 referendums were held, 40 of which passed. In the next year, 269 were held and 101 passed.[18]

Serrano Revisited

The Supreme Court's ruling in *Serrano* established the constitutional standards for California's school finance system. Because the case had not been tried in Superior Court, however, the factual basis of the plaintiffs' allegations had not been adjudicated. The Supreme Court therefore returned the case to the Los Angeles Superior Court for trial, which began in December 1972 with Judge Bernard Jefferson presiding. By this time, the system on trial was the one that had been amended by SB 90. The Supreme Court's ruling was unambiguous and the trial should have been straightforward. That was not to be the case, however, in part because of a ruling of the U.S. Supreme Court in *San Antonio Independent School System v. Rodriguez.*[19]

---

[18]California State Department of Education (1976).

[19]Elmore and McLaughlin (1982) describe this case in detail.

The Supreme Court that heard *Rodriguez* was different from the one that had launched the egalitarian revolution. Earl Warren had been replaced as Chief Justice by Warren Burger, and three other Nixon appointees had joined the court. Although the Burger Court expanded equal protection in some areas, such as gender discrimination, it halted the expansion of activities that were considered fundamental rights. Klarman (1991) argued that the court feared that further expansion would essentially involve it in "judicial wealth redistribution." A prime example of this new attitude was the court's ruling in *Rodriguez*. The *Rodriquez* lawyers argued that *Brown v. Board of Education* established education as a fundamental right. The court rejected this argument, concluding that education was not a fundamental right because it was not explicitly mentioned in the Constitution. This conclusion freed the lawyer representing the State of Texas from satisfying the standard of strict scrutiny. He was left only with the less-challenging task of showing that the Texas system bore some rational relationship to a legitimate state purpose. He argued that local control was the legitimate state purpose. The court accepted his argument and ruled that the system was constitutional.

The *Rodriguez* decision undercut the ruling of the California Supreme Court in *Serrano*. The California court had ruled that the state's system violated the equal protection clause of the Fourteenth Amendment. In a footnote to its decision, the court wrote that the violation of that clause must also entail a violation of related sections of the state Constitution. Its argument, however, focused exclusively on the U.S. Constitution. In the trial in Los Angeles Superior Court, the *Serrano* lawyers countered the *Rodriguez* ruling by arguing that although education was not mentioned in the U.S. Constitution, it was explicitly mentioned in the California Constitution. Although education may not be a fundamental right for federal purposes, it was a fundamental right in California.

In his decision, Judge Jefferson endorsed this argument, in effect dismissing *Rodriguez*. He then followed the *Serrano* decision to its logical conclusion. Senate Bill 90 moved the system in the right direction but had not gone far enough. Revenue limits would not converge fast enough, and that convergence could be vitiated by voter overrides. Judge Jefferson described how equal protection was violated in a number of specific instances, the most prominent of which was:

> Wealth-related disparities between school districts in per-pupil expenditures, apart from the categorical special needs programs, that are not designed to, and will not reduce to insignificant differences, which mean amounts considerably less than $100.00 per pupil, within a maximum period of six years from the date of entry of this Judgment.[20]

In effect, Judge Jefferson described an objective standard for determining the constitutionality of California's system. Differences across districts in spending per pupil could not be significantly related to differences in property wealth. In particular, these wealth-related differences should be less than $100 per pupil. Larger differences in spending per pupil would be constitutional if they were due to differences in the distribution of state categorical aid or other factors unrelated to wealth. There was now a concrete and specific standard against which future reforms could be measured.

The California Supreme Court endorsed Judge Jefferson's ruling in 1976 by a vote of four to three, which was closer than the 1971 decision of six to one. The change was due to two new justices appointed by

---

[20]*Serrano v. Priest*, 18 Cal. 3d 728; 557 P.2d 929; 135 Cal. Rptr. 345; hereafter *Serrano II*.

Governor Reagan, both of whom voted with the lone dissenter in the original ruling. Writing for the majority, Justice Sullivan acknowledged that the *Rodriguez* decision had undercut the original *Serrano* ruling. He pointed out, however, that the original ruling was also based on the California Constitution, quoting extensively from the footnote to that effect. He then endorsed the plaintiffs' argument that although education was not mentioned in the U.S. Constitution and was thus not a fundamental right for federal purposes, it was explicitly mentioned in the California Constitution and was therefore a fundamental right for state purposes.

The two Reagan appointees, Justice Richardson and Justice Clark, wrote dissents to this decision. From today's perspective, Justice Clark's dissent is particularly interesting because it discusses alternatives to the current system. In articulating the fiscal neutrality principle, Coons, Clune, and Sugarman had been careful to avoid advocating a particular alternative. They stressed that there were many options that would satisfy fiscal neutrality and that it was the legislature, not the courts, that should choose from among those options. In his dissent, Justice Clark measured three of the options that would satisfy fiscal neutrality against three desirable goals: equality, local control, and fiscal responsibility. He argued that none of the three options would achieve each of the three goals and that the current system represented a reasonable balance among those goals.

One option considered by Justice Clark was power-equalization, which appeared to him to be the option implicitly preferred by the majority of the court. Under power-equalization, districts with the same tax rates would have the same revenue per pupil, with the state making up the difference between a district's total revenue and the revenue it receives by applying its chosen rate to its own tax base. In evaluating this system, Justice Clark focused on a fundamental flaw in the fiscal neutrality principle. He argued that the revenue raised by a particular tax rate is not the proper measure of fiscal neutrality. The proper measure is the cost to taxpayers of achieving a certain level of spending per pupil. The two measures are not the same, as the following example illustrates. Imagine a community consisting entirely of residential property that was taxed to support its schools. Now suppose that property values were to double in the community. The community could raise the same level of property tax revenue with a tax rate that is half as much. Does this mean that the cost to taxpayers is half as much? No. Every taxpayer is paying exactly the same tax bill as before. The tax rate necessary to achieve a certain level of revenue per pupil does not measure the cost to taxpayers of achieving that level.

There are several other cases in which a strict application of fiscal neutrality leads to questionable results. One involves differences in the number of children per family. Suppose two communities have identical tax bases, but one has more school children per family. It will have a lower assessed value per pupil, and thus, under power-equalization, it will receive more state aid per pupil. Yet one could argue that differences in the number of children per family should not lead to differences in state aid per pupil.

Soon after the Supreme Court's ruling, the legislature began the task of designing a system that would satisfy the courts. The outcome was Assembly Bill 65, which passed in the fall of 1977.[21] The bill represented a movement away from the effort to equalize district revenue

---

[21]Mockler and Hayward (1978) describe AB 65.

and toward equalizing the assessed value of districts. It retained the revenue limit system introduced in SB 90 but added a power-equalization scheme, referred to as the Guaranteed Yield Program. Although AB 65 did not eliminate the right of voters to override their district's revenue limit, it did subject those overrides to power-equalization.

AB 65 represented the collective efforts of legislators and others to fashion a politically feasible response to *Serrano*. Although these efforts resulted in a much stronger response than SB 90, they pale in comparison to the actions taken by the voters one year later.

Proposition 13

Less than a month before AB 65 was to take effect, California voters approved Proposition 13, thus taking the step that the legislature was either too wise or too timid to attempt. In doing so, voters took away from school districts and other local governments the power to set their own property tax rates, imposing a limit on the sum of all local tax rates of 1 percent of assessed value. Proposition 13 also gave the state legislature the authority to allocate property tax revenue among local governments. This provision essentially turned the local property tax into a statewide tax. Ironically, a statewide property tax was one of the options initially proposed as a response to *Serrano*, but it was considered too radical to be seriously entertained.[22]

A deeper irony is that the state legislature's response to *Serrano* may have paved the way for Proposition 13, an argument advanced by Fischel

---

[22]In 1970, the Legislative Analyst, Alan Post, had proposed a statewide property tax on nonresidential property as a response to concerns about school finance equity. See Elmore and McLaughlin (1982), p. 76.

(1996). During the 1970s, housing prices in California rose rapidly, increasing assessments and property taxes. School districts were slow to reduce property tax rates to offset these assessment increases, partly because higher assessments were reducing their foundation aid, a process referred to as slippage. Of course, the state legislature could have acted more aggressively to counteract slippage by adjusting the foundation formula. It chose not to do so, Fischel argues, because it knew that a response to *Serrano* that would satisfy both the courts and the voters would also be expensive. In the short run, slippage helped the state accumulate a surplus that it could spend on an adequate response to *Serrano*. The voters saw that they were paying more taxes without receiving more services, and they voted to reduce those taxes.

Proposition 13 also changed the way property values were assessed. If a property was sold, it was assessed at 100 percent of its market value, instead of 25 percent, as was the case before Proposition 13. From that point forward, the assessed value of a property was to change as market value changed, with the exception that it could never increase by more than 2 percent per year until it was sold again, at which point it would be reassessed at market value. Consequently, a property could never be assessed at more than 100 percent of market value, implying that its tax rate could never be more than 1 percent of market value.[23] In contrast, the average property tax rate in 1977–78 was 10.68 percent of assessed value,[24] which was equivalent to a tax rate of 2.5 percent of market value.

---

[23]In addition, the assessed values of all properties were rolled back to 1975–76 market values. See O'Sullivan, Sexton, and Sheffrin (1995) for an analysis of this assessment system.

[24]Doerr (May 1998), p. 3.

As a result of these changes, property tax revenue fell 57 percent in the year after Proposition 13 was passed.[25]

The initiative itself was passed in June 1978, giving the state legislature a mere three weeks to enact the necessary legislation for the next fiscal year. The result was Senate Bill 154, a temporary one-year provision, which turned out to have the basic elements of the long-run implementation of Proposition 13. The key issue was the allocation among local governments of the property tax revenue raised under the new 1 percent tax rate. The bill allocated property tax revenue to each local government in proportion to its average revenue over the previous three years.[26]

To offset the decline in property tax revenue, the state legislature increased state aid to each local government. This allocation is described and analyzed in Shires (1999). Cities and counties received enough state aid to bring their total revenue to 90 percent of its previous level. In the case of school districts, however, the legislature saw SB 154 as an opportunity to move closer to compliance with the *Serrano* mandate. The mechanism was already in place in the form of revenue limits. In the days before Proposition 13, the revenue limit was a limit on the sum of property tax revenue and state aid, state aid was allocated according to the foundation formula, and thus the revenue limit became a limit on a district's property tax revenue. After Proposition 13, SB 154 determined a district's property tax revenue. Accordingly, the state legislature used

---

[25]O'Sullivan, Sexton, and Sheffrin (1995), p. 6.

[26]In subsequent legislation, AB 8, property tax revenue was allocated site by site. Property tax revenue generated from each parcel was allocated to local governments based on their revenue from that parcel before Proposition 13.

each district's revenue limit to determine its state aid. A district's state aid was the difference between its revenue limit and the property tax revenue allocated by SB 154.

Proposition 13 essentially turned the revenue limit system on its ear. Before the proposition, state aid was determined by a formula, and the revenue limit determined a district's property tax revenue. Voters could override that limit, however. After the proposition, the district's property tax revenue was determined by formula, and the revenue limit determined state aid. The proposition also eliminated voter overrides, thereby closing an important loophole in the revenue limit system.

Proposition 13 also shored up another weakness in the revenue limit system. A district's revenue no longer depended on the decisions its voters made about their tax rate. Instead, the district's property tax revenue was determined through SB 154, and the state filled in the rest of the revenue to get each district to its revenue limit. In that way, low-spending districts were automatically lifted to their revenue limits. Because the state legislature determined each district's revenue limit, it now determined its revenue as well.

Under SB 154, all districts received a one-time cut in revenue limits, as the state struggled to adjust to lower tax revenue after Proposition 13. However, the state implemented differential cuts, continuing the convergence in revenue limits initiated by SB 90. For districts with high revenue limits, limits were cut by 15 percent. For those with low limits, the cut was 9 percent. The cuts for other districts were between 9 percent and 15 percent, depending on their current limits.

The long-term implementation of Proposition 13 came in Assembly Bill 8, which the legislature passed in 1979. AB 8 changed the allocation of property tax revenue in SB 154 by shifting some revenue from school districts to cities, counties, and special districts.[27] However, because the bill continued to allocate state aid to school districts according to their revenue limits, this shift in property tax revenue did not diminish the total revenue of school districts. The decrease in their property tax revenue was automatically made up by an increase in state aid, financed through state general revenue. In effect, the property tax shift was a distribution of state general revenue to cities, counties, and special districts. AB 8 also continued the practice of increasing revenue limits at lower rates for districts with higher limits. For example, for 1980–81, a large unified district with a revenue limit of $1,500 per pupil received a 10 percent increase in its limit while a similar district with a revenue limit of $2,000 received a 4.25 percent increase.[28]

Although Proposition 13 tightened revenue limits, a few districts were still not held to them. This occurred when a district's property tax revenue exceeded is revenue limit. In such cases, the district still received basic aid from the state of $120 per unit of ADA and retained property tax revenue in excess of its limit. In 1992–93, there were 45 of these basic aid districts, enrolling approximately 2 percent of California students.[29]

---

[27]Doerr (May 1998), p. 24.

[28]Goldfinger (1980), p. 14. Whether a district was classified as high revenue or low revenue depended on its type and size. There were six classifications: elementary school districts with less than 101 average daily attendance (ADA), elementary school districts with more than 100 ADA, high school districts with less than 301 ADA, high school districts with more than 300 ADA, unified districts with less than 1,501 ADA, and unified districts with more than 1,500 ADA.

[29]The five largest basic aid districts were Newport Mesa Unified, San Luis Coastal Unified, Palo Alto Unified, Fremont Union High, and San Mateo Union High. Newport Mesa had 15,000 students; each of the others had between 7,000 and 8,000 students. In 1989–90, the median of revenue limit funds per pupil for unified districts was $3,108. Palo Alto Unified exceeded that median by more than $1,000 per pupil, San

Despite the strengthening of SB 90 brought about by Proposition 13, the *Serrano* plaintiffs took the state back to the Los Angeles Superior Court in 1983. In essence, the trial was a compliance hearing to determine whether the state had met the standards of the Jefferson decision. The key issue in the trial was the interpretation of Judge Jefferson's $100 band for spending per pupil. The defense argued that the band was one of many ways of measuring inequality, and it presented several other measures. It also argued that the band, if used at all, ought to be adjusted for inflation. The plaintiffs, on the other hand, argued for a literal interpretation of Judge Jefferson's ruling. Judge Olsen favored the interpretation offered by the defense. In his opinion, he wrote that

> Undue emphasis on the $100 figure would be inappropriate. Rather, both fact and law lead this court to interpret the judgment to require elimination of all but "insignificant differences."[30]

He interpreted the $100 band as an illustration of insignificant differences, not as the definition of that phrase. He also emphasized that times had changed since the original ruling and that an apt illustration in 1973 was not necessarily apt 10 years later. He concluded that

> It is this court's view that the proper standard for testing compliance with the judgment is whether the Legislature has done all that is reasonably feasible to reduce disparities in per-pupil expenditures to insignificant differences. As is discussed, the state has met this standard and surpassed it.[31]

Luis Coastal by more than $700, and Newport Mesa by about $300. Fremont and San Mateo exceeded the median for high school districts by less than $400 per pupil.

[30] *Serrano v. Priest,* 200 Cal. App. 3d 897; 1986 Cal. App. LEXIS 1586; 226 Cal. Rptr. 584.

[31] *Serrano v. Priest,* 200 Cal. App. 3d 897; 1986 Cal. App. LEXIS 1586; 226 Cal. Rptr. 584.

During the hearing, the *Serrano* plaintiffs also raised concerns about the distribution of categorical aid. In addressing those concerns, Judge Olsen reinforced the Jefferson decision. He declared that categorical programs are not covered by the *Serrano* judgment, writing "These programs are not wealth-related, and they are not, in any event, discriminatory." Judge Olsen's decision was upheld on appeal and a settlement was finally reached between plaintiffs and defendants in 1989.

The revenue limit system, with some modification, continues to the present day. In 1983, the state discontinued the differential growth rates in revenue limits and began increasing each school district's limit by the same dollar amount per pupil. The "squeeze" factor was eliminated in tacit recognition that enough convergence had been achieved to satisfy the courts. Despite this modification, there were still forces causing convergence in limits. First, because every district received the same dollar per ADA increase in its base revenue limit, districts with low limits received higher percentage increases than districts with high limits. Second, if a district's revenue limit was more than 5 percent above the state average, the revenue limit funds resulting from growth in enrollment above the district's 1982–83 level were determined by the state average revenue limit per pupil instead of the district's revenue limit per pupil.[32] Finally, the state has periodically raised the revenue limits of districts below the state average. For this purpose, the state spent $21 million in both 1985–86 and 1986–87, $73 million in 1989–90, and $163 million in 1995–96.[33]

---

[32]This provision was in effect from 1982–83 to 1997–98, when it was eliminated in SB 727.

[33]Goldfinger (1996), p. 11.

The state also adjusted the revenue limits of certain districts as it brought in new programs and phased out old ones. An example of the first type of adjustment was Senate Bill 813, enacted in 1983.[34] The purpose of the bill was to encourage districts to devote more resources to instruction. The state increased the revenue limits of districts that lengthened their academic year or raised their minimum salary for newly hired teachers. An example of the second type of adjustment was the elimination of Urban Impact Aid, a categorical program primarily benefiting large urban districts. When the program was phased out in 1989–90, the state rolled the funds received by districts into their revenue limits.

The cumulative effect of revenue limit growth rates is represented in Figure 3.3. The figure shows the percentage increase from 1974–75 to

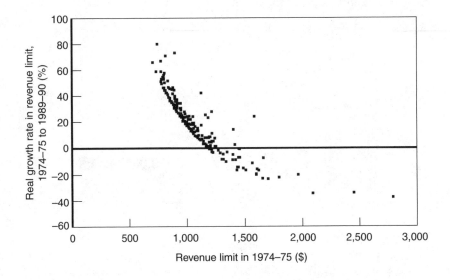

Figure 3.3—Growth Rate in Revenue Limits: Unified Districts

---

[34]SB 813 is described in detail in Picus (1991b).

1989–90 in the revenue limits of unified districts. The 1989–90 revenuelimits are adjusted for inflation, using the consumer price index (CPI), so the growth rates are in real terms. Districts with very low limits in 1974–75 had increases exceeding 50 percent, whereas districts with high limits had decreases in their limits, adjusted for inflation. Elementary and secondary school districts experienced similar differentials in revenue limit growth. Those growth rates are depicted in Appendix Figures B.1 and B.2.

The differential growth rates in revenue limits produced a gradual convergence in limits, a convergence depicted in Figure 3.4. The gray area in the figure is the 90 percent band for revenue limit per pupil. Five percent of students attended districts in which the revenue limit per pupil exceeded this band, 5 percent attended districts in which the limit was below this band, and the remaining 90 percent attended districts where the limit was within this band. The upper and lower limits of the

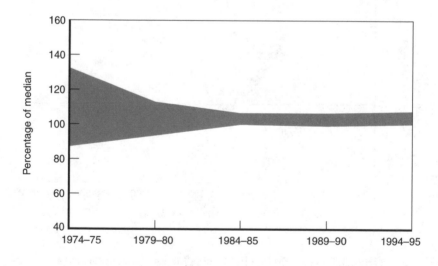

Figure 3.4—The 90 Percent Band for Revenue Limits: Unified Districts

band are expressed relative to the median revenue limit per pupil in each year. For example, in 1974–75, 5 percent of students were in districts where the revenue limit per pupil was less than 86 percent of the median. In contrast, by 1994–95, this bottom limit of the band had increased to 99 percent of the median. A similar convergence occurred for the upper limit. In 1974–75, 5 percent of students attended districts where the revenue limit per pupil was more than 30 percent of the median. By 1994–95, the upper limit of the band had declined to 7 percent of the median.

As revenue limits converged, there was also a shift in the composition of school district revenue. As Figure 3.5 illustrates, property tax revenue declined sharply because of Proposition 13. In 1977–78, the year just before the passage of Proposition 13, property tax revenue constituted 58 percent of all revenue. One year later, it had fallen to 27 percent of revenue. The gap was filled by state aid. In 1969–70, aid to school

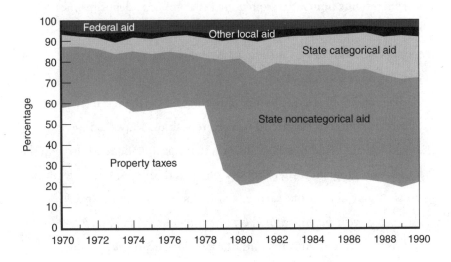

Figure 3.5—Composition of School District Revenue, 1970–1990

districts through the state's foundation program constituted 29 percent of all revenue. It had fallen to 23 percent of all revenue by 1972–73, in part as a result of slippage. SB 90 increased the foundation level, and state noncategorical aid rose to 28 percent of revenue in 1973–74. This increase was quickly undone by the rise in property values in the mid-1970s, causing a new round of slippage. By 1977–78, state noncategorical aid had returned to 23 percent of all revenue. By the next year, however, that relatively small decline had been reversed as the state made up the loss in property tax revenue from Proposition 13. In 1978–79, state noncategorical aid was 53 percent of revenue, a level that was sustained through the rest of the 1970s and the 1980s.

This share fell somewhat during the recession in the early 1990s. In response to budgetary problems, the state shifted some property tax revenue from cities, counties, and special districts to schools, thereby decreasing the amount of state general funds necessary to fund school district revenue limits. It also required that counties deposit some property tax revenue that had previously gone to cities, counties, and special districts into an Educational Revenue Augmentation Fund, which was distributed to schools.[35]

Figure 3.5 illustrates another important trend, the rise in state categorical aid. For the period before Proposition 13, we define state categorical aid as aid to school districts that was not allocated through the foundation program. After Proposition 13 and SB 154, state categorical aid is all state aid not included in a district's revenue limit. In 1969–70, state categorical aid constituted 6 percent of all revenue; by 1996–97, it had risen to 23 percent. In contrast, state noncategorical aid plus

---

[35]Legislative Analyst's Office (1996).

property tax revenue—the sum that would become subject to revenue limits—constituted 87 percent of all revenue in 1969–70. By 1996–97, that sum had fallen to 69 percent.

While revenue limit funds were becoming more equally distributed, they were also becoming a smaller fraction of total funds. Over time, equalization was applied to a smaller and smaller fraction of total revenue, leading to the question of whether total revenue was becoming more equally distributed. Figure 3.6 shows the change in the dispersion of total revenue per pupil across school districts. Total revenue comprises revenue limit funds, state categorical aid, federal aid, and other local revenue. The 90 percent band for total revenue per pupil—the band encompassing 90 percent of students in unified districts—shrank steadily from 1969–70 to 1984–85. According to Evans, Murray, and Schwab (1997), California ranked 45th among states in equality of spending per pupil in 1972. By 1987, it ranked 5th.

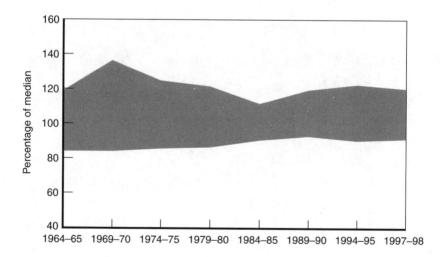

Figure 3.6—The 90 Percent Band for Total Revenue per Pupil: Unified Districts

From that point, however, the trend toward equality in total revenue was reversed. From 1984–85 through the 1990s, the 90 percent band for total revenue per pupil expanded considerably. This trend is in marked contrast to the trend for revenue limits, where dispersion declined to 1984–85 and then remained at that level through the 1990s. The difference between the two trends is due to state categorical aid, which grew steadily in the 1980s and 1990s and caused growing inequality in total revenue per pupil

The difference between the distribution of total revenue and revenue limits is a natural consequence of the "rational" system Stephen Sugarman may have envisioned in 1974. Under such a system, general revenue would be evenly distributed with additional revenue targeted for the special needs of disadvantaged children. How much state categorical aid is actually targeted for those needs? Figure 3.7 gives a partial answer. The figure shows the percentage of state categorical aid in each of three

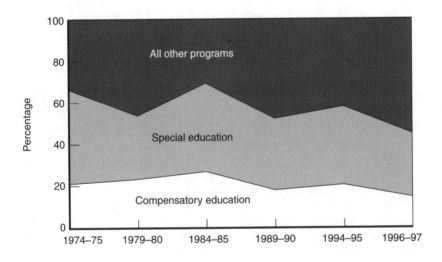

Figure 3.7—The Composition of State Categorical Programs

categories: compensatory education, special education, and all other programs. Compensatory education consists of programs designed specifically for disadvantaged students. In 1974–75, these programs were Bilingual Education and Educationally Disadvantaged Youth. In subsequent years, the programs included Urban Impact Aid, Economic Impact Aid, Court Ordered Desegregation, and Voluntary Desegregation. Over time, an average of about 20 percent of state categorical aid has been allocated to compensatory education. Chapter 4 examines these programs in more detail.

By their very nature, categorical programs are not distributed equally across school districts, giving each district an incentive to make sure that its special needs are known to the state legislature. As a consequence, school districts have become much more active in legislative lobbying. According to Elmore and McLaughlin (1982), the education lobby before the early 1970s consisted mainly of a union representing teachers, an association representing school superintendents, and an association representing school boards. Prompted by the legislature's response to *Serrano,* a few large school districts began to send lobbyists to Sacramento, a trend that has continued and expanded in scope. Figure 3.8 shows the growth in real expenditures of California school districts on legislative lobbyists, as reported to the Secretary of State. In several cases, districts are represented by their own lobbyists. In other cases, a group of districts is represented by an association. Those associations included the Association of Low Wealth Schools, the California Association of Large Suburban School Districts, Schools for Sound Finance, and the Small Districts Association. We have also included the lobbying expenditure of the Association of California School

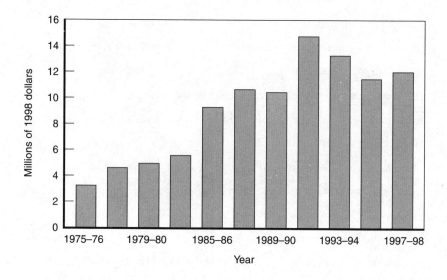

Figure 3.8—School District Expenditures on Legislative Lobbyists

Administrators, the California School Boards Association, and County Offices of Education.

Conclusion

The transformation from local to state finance was accomplished in three steps. In *Serrano v. Priest*, the California Supreme Court ruled that the existing system of local finance was unconstitutional. The second step was Senate Bill 90, which initiated revenue limits, giving the state some control over the property tax revenue of school districts. The final step was Proposition 13, which authorized the state to allocate property tax revenue and tightened the state's control over school finance. By the early 1980s, the state had gained direct control of 90 percent of school district revenue.

For the reform-minded lawyers who brought the *Serrano* suit, these events may have been disquieting. Yet the end result could not have been better suited to their ultimate objective. As Oates (1972) noted in his classic analysis of fiscal federalism, local finance has many good points, but an equitable allocation of resources is not usually counted among them. If wealth redistribution is the ultimate aim, finance at a higher level of government is an appropriate mechanism. *Serrano* made this possible. By moving public school finance to the state level, it opened the door for a substantial redistribution of educational resources.

State finance is not a sufficient condition for such redistribution, however. That outcome depends on the attitudes and actions of the state legislature. If it desires, the legislature can adjust revenue to direct money toward any district or group of students. Has the state legislature used its new control over school district revenues to address the needs of disadvantaged students? Chapter 4 examines this issue.

4. The Allocation of Revenues Under State Finance

By 1985, the state had nearly equalized the allocation of revenue limit funds across districts. Throughout the 1980s and 1990s, it also increased the share of all revenue allocated through state categorical programs. The share grew from about 6 percent of all revenue in 1970 to 15 percent in 1984–85 and to 20 percent in 1989–90—a level that was sustained through the 1990s. The courts did not require categorical aid to be equally distributed, thus giving the state much latitude in allocating revenue among school districts. Although revenue inequalities in 1970 mostly reflected local conditions and preferences, such inequalities in 1985 largely reflected the preferences of the state legislature.

As Chapter 3 showed, there were substantial inequalities under state finance. This chapter analyzes the sources of those inequalities and their relationship to the characteristics of children and their families. The chapter focuses on 1989–90 because the 1990 Census provides extensive family data in that year.

School Districts

The transformation in school finance had little effect on the institutions of public education. Most school districts, which remained the primary administrative units, had the same boundaries as in 1970. Some elementary and secondary school districts merged between 1969–70 and 1989–90. Because of these consolidations, the total number of elementary and secondary school districts fell by 109, and the number of unified districts increased by 41, leaving 1,010 districts overall. Unified districts enrolled 68 percent of students in 1989–90 and averaged more than 10,000 students per district. Many school districts were still small, however: 346 districts had fewer than 500 students, and 304 of these were elementary school districts.

State Categorical Programs

In 1992–93, the state funded 57 categorical programs, most of which were relatively small.[1] Table 4.1 lists the seven programs that spent more than $150 million each in 1989–90. Those programs accounted for 80 percent of all funds expended through categorical programs. The list excludes the incentive program for a longer school day and longer school year because funds for that program are allocated through district revenue limits.

Of the seven programs listed in Table 4.1, the easiest to describe is the State Lottery Program, which distributed funds from the state lottery

---

[1]Legislative Analyst's Office (1993).

Table 4.1

State Categorical Programs in 1989–90
(in $ millions)

Programs exceeding $150 million	
Special Education	1,078
State Lottery	765
Voluntary and Court Ordered Desegregation	460
Home to School Transportation	273
School Improvement	253
Economic Impact Aid	210
Supplemental Grants	169
Subtotal	3,208
All other grants and programs	678
Total	3,886

in proportion to district enrollment. In 1989–90, the average allocation was approximately $170 per pupil. Lottery revenue was virtually unrestricted; it could be spent on almost any purpose other than acquisition of property or construction.

In contrast, the most complex program was Special Education. In 1980, the state's program was overhauled by the Master Plan for Special Education.[2] Under that plan, the state partially reimbursed each district for the cost of its Special Education Program. The reimbursements were based on historical costs, specifically the expenditures of districts in 1979–80 adjusted for inflation. To illustrate how the program worked, imagine a district that identified 30 students to place in a separate, special education classroom. According to state guidelines, there should be 10 students in each special education classroom, so the district should have three special education classrooms. In 1979–80, it may have staffed

---

[2]This description of California's Special Education Program is based on Goldfinger (1996) and Legislative Analyst's Office, Department of Education, and Department of Finance (1995).

each classroom with a special education teacher and a teacher's aide. Their salaries, adjusted for inflation, were the basis for state reimbursement in 1989–90. The district was also reimbursed for support services for each classroom. This reimbursement was determined by multiplying the direct costs of the teacher and aide by the support ratio, which was the cost of support services identified in 1979–80 divided by the salary of the teacher and aide in the same year.

Although separate classrooms constituted a large part of the special education costs reimbursed by the state, there were other costs as well. These included the costs of speech therapists, psychologists, and other specialists who served special education students enrolled in regular classrooms for most of the school day. Districts were reimbursed for these expenses through a formula similar to that for separate classrooms. A district was also reimbursed for a portion of the costs of placing a student in a special school or agency outside the district.[3]

Each district was required to finance a portion of its special education expenses from its own general funds. These portions, referred to as the "local general fund contribution," were also based on district expenditures in 1979–80. In that year, each district funded its Special Education Program through a combination of state and local funds. The local general fund contribution was designed to perpetuate these ratios of state and local funding.

---

[3]Under the Master Plan, each district belonged to a Special Education Local Plan Area (SELPA). Each large district had its own SELPA. For smaller districts, a SELPA would typically contain several districts, and would coordinate the special education programs of its member districts.

The funding of special education involved many inequities.[4] The reimbursement rates varied dramatically from district to district. In 1993–94, the reimbursement rate for a special education classroom ranged from $22,100 to $56,500, and support ratios varied from 0 to 78 percent. The local general fund contribution also differed widely across districts. In 1993–94, these contributions ranged from $0 to more than $300 per pupil. General fund contributions were particularly difficult for districts that funded generous Special Education Programs in the 1970s through their own property tax revenue. They were required to maintain their large contributions from their general funds even as those funds were equalized across districts by the revenue limits. Furthermore, the state reduced its contribution shortly after enacting the Master Plan, leaving school districts with an even larger share of special education costs.[5]

The Home to School Transportation Program provided funding to transport pupils to and from school. Through 1983–84, separate allocations were made for special education students and for other students. The two allocations were combined until 1992–93 and then separated again. The program allocated funds to districts on the basis of their costs, though it reimbursed districts for only a portion of their costs.[6]

The Court Ordered Desegregation Program also reimbursed districts for specific costs.[7] Most of the funds in this program were allocated to

---

[4]See Legislative Analyst's Office, Department of Education, and Department of Finance (1995).

[5]See Goldfinger (1996), p. 90.

[6]See Goldfinger (1996).

[7]The description of the Court Ordered Desegregation Program is based on Department of Finance (1987).

school districts with a court ordered desegregation plan or court approved consent decree. The state reimbursed districts for all costs deemed to be consistent with these plans. Table 4.2 lists the reimbursements to districts in 1989–90.

The program originated in 1978–79, the year after Proposition 13 was enacted. Three districts (Los Angeles, San Bernardino, and San Diego Unified) had been operating under court ordered desegregation plans, which they financed through "permissive override" property tax rates authorized by the state legislature as explained in Chapter 2. Because these rates were invalidated by the passage of Proposition 13, the state assumed the responsibility for financing the plans. In the initial year, the state appropriated $81 million for this purpose, with $71 million going to Los Angeles Unified. Since that time, eight other districts have entered the program. In addition, 30 districts participated in a Voluntary Desegregation Program, for which $74 million was appropriated in 1989–90. Seven of the districts in the court ordered

Table 4.2

Court Ordered Desegregation Program in 1989–90

District	Expenditure	Average Daily Attendance	Expenditure per Student
Bakersfield Unified	$3,063,839	23,585	$130
Los Angeles Unified	285,872,852	609,746	469
Palo Alto Unified	254,946	7,495	34
Ravenswood Elementary	50,398	3,660	14
Redwood City Elementary	15,512	7,654	2
San Bernardino Unified	7,080,239	39,033	181
San Diego Unified	39,313,777	119,314	329
San Francisco Unified	28,200,000	61,935	455
San Jose Unified	21,801,191	29,005	752
Sequoia Union High	91,862	6,266	15
Stockton Unified	2,243,174	31,849	70

program also received funds through the Voluntary Desegregation Program.

The cost of the program escalated rapidly. Between 1978 and 1990, the appropriations for Los Angeles Unified quadrupled, more than doubling in real terms. San Bernardino and San Diego had similar increases. Costs increased because school districts and the courts expanded the scope of activities included in their desegregation plans. Most plans adopted some version of the Racially Isolated Minority Schools (RIMS) Program, which was part of the original plan adopted by Los Angeles Unified. Under the program, a district could designate schools with a high percentage of minority students as being impractical to integrate by transferring students. The district would provide additional resources to those schools, mitigating the effects of segregation. Other costs of desegregation plans included staff development programs, computer purchases, and capital outlays for maintenance and upgrading of facilities. The Desegregation Cost Review Committee, organized by the Department of Finance, concluded that desegregation plans had evolved from activities targeting students affected by segregation to activities benefiting all students in a district.[8]

The rapid rise in the cost of desegregation programs prompted a change in the method for reimbursing district expenses. Under the provisions of AB 38, which was passed in 1985, districts were reimbursed for 100 percent of their desegregation expenses up to a limit equal to their actual expenses in 1984–85 adjusted for inflation and enrollment growth. They were reimbursed at the rate of 80 percent for any additional expenses. For the Voluntary Desegregation Program,

---

[8]Department of Finance (1987).

73

reimbursements were capped at 80 percent of costs in 1984–85, adjusted for inflation.

In large part, California's Desegregation Program evolved into a Compensatory Education Program. The other large compensatory program was Economic Impact Aid, which had its roots in the Education for Disadvantaged Youth Program adopted as part of SB 90 of 1972. Economic impact aid was allocated according to a complex formula.[9] In 1989–90, about 75 percent of the funds were allocated by the primary formula, which was designed to give the highest priority to maintaining previous allocations. First, the State Department of Education determined the "gross need" for funds by multiplying the number of children in the state receiving AFDC by the "average excess cost of education," which was $565 per pupil in 1989–90. The next step was to compute a measure of a district's need, which was the number of targeted students in the district multiplied by an "impaction" factor. The number of targeted students was the average of the number of students in AFDC families and the number of students living in poverty as determined by the Census. The impaction factor was an average of three indexes: (1) the percentage of limited-English proficiency students divided by the state average of this index, (2) the percentage of AFDC students divided by the state average of this index, and (3) an index of pupil transience, which was computed from the ratio of the district's average daily attendance and its total enrollment. The purpose of the impaction factor was to allocate more aid per student to districts with high concentrations of targeted students.

---

[9]This description of Economic Impact Aid is based on Legislative Analyst's Office (1987).

Based on this measure of need, each district was assigned a proportionate share of the state's "gross need," and each district's gross need was separated into two parts. The first part was met as a first priority. If a district's gross need exceeded the previous year's allocation, the first priority was the previous year's allocation. If its gross need fell short of the previous year's allocation, the first priority was its gross need, with the qualification that this first priority could never be less than 85 percent of its allocation the year before. After these first priorities were fulfilled, the rest of the funds were allocated according to "unmet" needs, which were the excess of gross needs over the previous year's allocation.

The second part of each district's gross need formula was commonly known as the "bounce file." It allocated funds to districts that did not have enough targeted students to qualify for funds under the primary formula. According to the parameters of this secondary formula for 1989–90, every district with at least one economically disadvantaged student received a minimum of $6,000. The formula then allocated the remaining funds in proportion to the number of AFDC children in the districts. In 1989–90, $54 million was allocated through the bounce file.

The School Improvement Program (SIP) was established in 1977 as part of AB 65, the school finance reform that was undercut by Proposition 13.[10] The program had its roots in the Early Childhood Education Program, which was created as part of the earlier school finance reform, SB 90. The goal of the School Improvement Program was to encourage schools to undertake a fundamental reassessment of their needs. Participation in the program was voluntary, but participating schools were required to set up a School Site Council

---

[10]This account of the School Improvement Program is based on Berman, Weiler Associates (1983).

consisting of teachers, administrators, and parents. Each council adopted a plan for addressing the needs of its school, and the plans were submitted to the State Department of Education for funding.

The state placed few constraints on the use of SIP funds. They could not be used for purchasing capital, reducing class sizes, or supplanting other school resources. In practice, elementary schools tended to use their SIP funds to hire teachers' aides. Secondary schools often created special programs in reading and writing, hiring specialists to staff those programs. Once a school's plan was approved for funding, the school essentially had an entitlement, which was renewed annually.

The last of the large categorical programs was the Supplemental Grants Program, sometimes referred to as categorical equalization.[11] Supplemental grants were allocated to districts that received few funds from other categorical programs. To determine its entitlement, a district summed its revenues from both its revenue limit and 26 other categorical programs. If its sum per pupil was less than the statewide average, it received a supplemental grant equal to that difference up to a maximum of $100 per pupil.

Other Local Revenue

Another source of district revenue was local revenue that was not included in a district's revenue limit. In 1989–90, this revenue amounted to $709 million—about 4 percent of total revenue. Table 4.3 lists the major categories of this revenue. Perhaps the most interesting category is parcel taxes, which resemble property taxes in that they are levied on parcels of real property. They differ from property taxes in that

---

[11]The Supplemental Grants Program is described in Picus, Odden, and Kim (1992).

Table 4.3

Local Revenue Other Than the Property Tax: 1989–90
(in $ millions)

Parcel taxes	24
Leases and rentals	64
Interagency revenue	75
Miscellaneous sales, fees, and taxes	127
Interest	269
All other local revenue	150
Total	709

they are levied on the parcel itself instead of on the value of the parcel and its improvements. In 1989–90, 27 school districts levied a parcel tax. The lowest tax rate was $25 per parcel, and the highest was $250 per parcel. The Berkeley Unified School District levied a parcel tax that depended on the area of the parcel and whether it was used for commercial or residential purposes.

Parcel taxes were an offspring of Proposition 13. The main purpose of the initiative was to limit the tax on property values. In addition, Section 4 of the proposition required that "special taxes" be approved by a two-thirds vote of the electorate. Although it is natural to interpret that provision as limiting the ability of local governments to make up their property tax losses with other taxes, the initiative did not define what constituted a special tax. One possible definition of a special tax is one that targets a particular group of taxpayers. Under this definition, a tax with a wide incidence is a general tax and does not require a two-thirds majority. The City and County of San Francisco appealed to that interpretation when it raised its payroll tax in 1980 to pay for improvements at a municipally owned hospital—a tax increase that was approved by only a majority of voters.

A second possible definition of a special tax is one that is earmarked for a particular use. The state legislature was apparently following that definition in 1979 when it gave local governments the authority to levy a parcel tax for police and fire protection. The legislation was very specific about the uses of the tax revenue and required that the tax be approved by two-thirds of the electorate. This definition was adopted by the California Supreme Court in its 1982 decision in *San Francisco v. Farrell*.[12] The court invalidated the payroll tax increase enacted by San Francisco because it was a "special" tax, earmarked for a particular purpose, and thus requiring a two-thirds majority.

This ruling had serious implications for school districts. Under the court's definition, taxes for school districts were special taxes because they were earmarked for schools. Thus, Section 4 of Proposition 13 gave school districts the right to levy parcel taxes but also required that such taxes be approved by a two-thirds vote. The first parcel tax was enacted in 1983.[13]

The Allocation of Revenue Across Districts

Every source of local revenue has its own rationale, as does every state categorical program. Taken together, these individual sources and programs determine the allocation of total revenue across school districts. Chapter 3 showed that although total revenues were more equally distributed across school districts in 1989–90 than in 1969–70, there was

---

[12] *City and County of San Francisco v. Farrell,* 184 Cal. Rptr. 713, U 32 Cal. ed 47, 648 P.2d 935.

[13] The definition of "special" tax was clarified by Proposition 218, which passed in November 1996. According to the proposition, "special tax means any tax imposed for specific purposes . . ." and all special taxes require a two-thirds majority. The proposition also defines school districts as special districts, which can levy only special taxes.

still considerable inequality in 1989–90. This section investigates the sources of that inequality.

Table 4.4 lists unified school districts grouped by quartiles of revenue per pupil. Of all students attending unified school districts in 1989–90, one-quarter attended a district in which total revenue per pupil was less than $4,071. These districts constitute the first quartile in the table. Among unified districts, state categorical programs were the primary cause of inequality. The difference in total revenue per pupil between the first and fourth quartile was $1,093. The difference in state categorical revenue was $755—70 percent of the total difference.

Categorical aid is not as important in explaining the differences among elementary school districts, however. As Table 4.5 demonstrates, the difference between the fourth and first quartiles for total revenue per pupil was $818, whereas the difference in state categorical aid was only

Table 4.4

Revenue Sources of Total Revenue per Pupil, by Quartile: Unified Districts in 1989–90
(in dollars)

Quartile	Revenue Limit Funds per Pupil	State Categorical Aid per Pupil	Federal Aid per Pupil	Other Local Revenue per Pupil	Total Revenue per Pupil
First quartile 0–4,071	3,065	660	114	125	3,964
Second quartile 4,072–4,228	3,091	759	159	139	4,148
Third quartile 4,229–4,894	3,162	909	249	160	4,480
Fourth quartile 4,895 and above	3,219	1,415	279	144	5,057

Table 4.5

Revenue Sources of Total Revenue per Pupil, by Quartile: Elementary School Districts in 1989–90
(in dollars)

	Revenue Limit Funds per Pupil	State Categorical Aid per Pupil	Federal Aid per Pupil	Other Local Revenue per Pupil	Total Revenue per Pupil
First quartile 0–3,695	2,797	592	97	97	3,583
Second quartile 3,696–3,861	2,824	680	153	118	3,774
Third quartile 3,862–4,016	2,859	749	187	134	3,929
Fourth quartile 4,017 and above	3,084	787	237	293	4,401

$195. The difference in revenue limit funds is larger than the difference in categorical aid ($287 compared to $195), although differences in revenue limits account for only 35 percent of the total. The same conclusion holds for high school districts, as demonstrated in Appendix Table C.1.

Chapter 3 described the first large categorical program in the 1970s—the result of the political compromise that led to the passage of SB 90. The Education for Disadvantaged Youths Program benefited several large urban districts, which were also high-wealth, high-spending districts that would be adversely affected by revenue limits. In that instance, categorical aid offset some of the revenue those districts would lose as revenue limits converged over time. If this pattern persisted through the 1970s and 1980s, state categorical aid would have continued to flow in greater proportions to districts with higher revenue limits in 1974–75.

Table 4.6 provides some evidence consistent with that hypothesis. The table gives state categorical aid per pupil for districts separated into quartiles by their 1974–75 revenue limits. Of the students attending unified districts in 1989–90, one-quarter attended a district in which the 1974–75 revenue limit was less than $893. The second quartile has higher categorical aid per pupil than the first, and the third has higher aid than the second. This pattern is consistent with the idea that categorical aid was used to offset losses resulting from revenue limits. However, the highest quartile has lower categorical aid than either the second or third quartile, which is not consistent with the hypothesis.

The third quartile in Table 4.6 is unusual in two ways. The first is evident from the table itself; categorical aid per student is much higher in this quartile than in any other quartile. The third quartile is also unusual because of its composition. It contains the two largest unified districts, Los Angeles and San Diego, and they constitute nearly 90 percent of the enrollment in the quartile. The high average of state categorical aid per pupil in the third quartile is entirely due to those two districts.

Table 4.6

**State Categorical Aid per Pupil, by Quartiles of 1974–75
Revenue Limits: Unified Districts in 1989–90**
(in dollars)

Quartile	State Categorical Aid per Pupil
First quartile 0–893	734
Second quartile 893–945	855
Third quartile 945–987	1,352
Fourth quartile 987 and above	834

Categorical aid averaged $1,538 per pupil in Los Angeles and $1,337 per pupil in San Diego.

Are Los Angeles and San Diego special cases, or did all large districts benefit from state categorical aid? Table 4.7 lists the nine large districts identified in Chapter 2. These districts represent the full range of revenue limits. Among unified districts ranked by their 1974–75 revenue limits, Garden Grove and Fresno were in the first quartile; San Juan, Sacramento, and San Diego were in the second quartile; Los Angeles was in the third; and Long Beach, Oakland, and San Francisco were in the top quartile.

Despite the equalization of revenue limit sources among these districts, there were still large differences in total revenue per pupil. The differences were almost entirely due to the distribution of categorical aid, which tended to offset the convergence in revenue limits. Garden Grove had the lowest revenue limit in 1974–75 and the lowest total revenue per

Table 4.7

Revenue per Pupil in 1989–90 in Districts with More Than 50,000 Students in 1969–70
(in dollars)

District	Revenue Limit in 1974–75	Revenue Limit Sources	State Categorical Aid	Total Revenue
Garden Grove	843	3,026	754	4,178
Fresno	890	3,160	866	4,352
San Juan	893	3,137	898	4,272
Sacramento	896	3,111	787	4,309
San Diego	911	3,087	1,337	4,894
Los Angeles	972	3,146	1,538	5,003
Long Beach	1,112	3,033	823	4,228
Oakland	1,117	3,183	905	4,486
San Francisco	1,450	3,209	1,088	4,923

pupil in 1989–90. San Francisco had the highest revenue limit in 1974–75 and the second highest total revenue per pupil in 1989–90. San Juan and Sacramento had revenue limits below the median for the nine districts in 1974–75 and total revenue below the median in 1989–90. Los Angeles and Oakland were above the median in both revenue limits and total revenue. The only real exception to this pattern is Long Beach, which had the third highest revenue limit in 1974–75 and the second lowest revenue per pupil in 1989–90.

Comparisons among large unified districts are less significant, however, than the comparison of these districts with smaller unified districts. State finance was relatively beneficial to large unified districts. In 1969–70, five of the nine largest districts had revenue per pupil below the median for all unified districts. By 1989–90, only two had revenue per pupil below the median. In 1969–70, Garden Grove, San Juan, and Sacramento were in the bottom quartile of districts. By 1989–90, none of the nine districts were in the bottom quartile.

One possible theory explaining the higher categorical aid received by large school districts concerns representation in the state legislature.[14] Larger districts are better represented in the legislature than smaller districts. Voters living within the boundaries of Los Angeles Unified elect several legislators, but a small district may share a legislator with several other districts. The expense of a legislative lobbyist is also a smaller percentage of a large district's budget than it is for a small district.

Another possible explanation for the higher categorical aid received by large districts is that those districts may have special needs. Many large urban districts have high concentrations of poor families who may

---

[14]Timar (1994) examines the political forces affecting the distribution of categorical aid.

have exceptional educational needs. The next section addresses the relationship between need and the allocation of categorical aid by investigating the distribution of revenues by family income.

The Distribution of Total Revenue Across Income Groups

Did state finance allocate more revenue to districts with a higher percentage of poor families? To address that question, we collected data on family income from the School District Data Book—a special tabulation of the 1990 Census that aggregated data to the school district level. The Data Book for California included only 800 of California's 1,010 districts, excluding districts in 12 of California's 58 counties.[15] The included districts constituted 94 percent of California's average daily attendance in 1989–90.

Figure 4.1 shows the distribution of revenue per pupil for three different income groups: low-income families, middle-income families, and high-income families. The distribution is very similar across groups. Low-income families, which constituted 28 percent of all families, are those with an annual income of less than $20,000. Middle-income families had annual incomes between $20,000 and $60,000 and constituted 44 percent of families. High-income families are the top 28 percent of families—those with annual incomes in excess of $60,000. About 40 percent of each group lived in a district with per pupil revenue between 95 percent and 105 percent of the median. Low-income families were more likely to live in high-revenue districts than were middle- and high-income families, but the differences are small.

---

[15]The excluded counties are Butte, El Dorado, Humboldt, Kings, Madera, Monterey, Napa, San Benito, Santa Barbara, Siskiyou, Tehama, and Trinity.

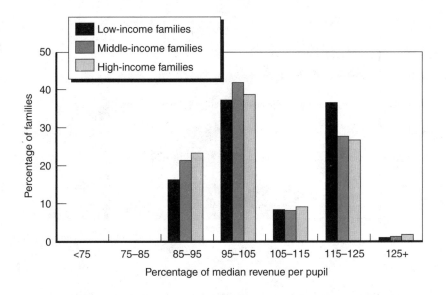

**Figure 4.1—Distribution of Revenue per Pupil, by Family Income:
Unified Districts in 1989–90**

How has state finance affected the distribution of revenues by
income group? In particular, how does the distribution of revenue in
1970 compare with the distribution in 1990? A comparison of Figure
2.11 and Figure 4.1 reveals some differences but also one important
similarity. Within income groups, there was more equality in revenues
per pupil in 1990 than in 1970—a result of equalizing revenues across
districts. Across income groups, there were fewer changes. As in 1970,
the distribution of revenue in 1990 was very similar across income
groups.

Chapter 2 also examined the distribution of revenue per pupil by the
race and ethnicity of students. Figure 4.2 provides a comparable
breakdown for 1989–90. Almost 40 percent of black and Hispanic
students lived in districts where revenue per pupil was more than 115

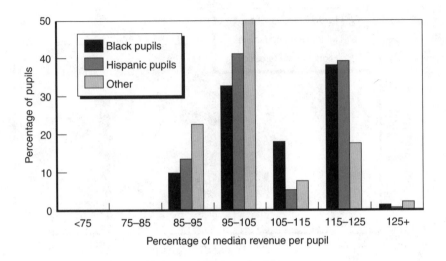

Figure 4.2—Distribution of Revenue per Pupil, by Race and Ethnicity: Unified Districts in 1969–70

percent of the median. In contrast, less than 20 percent of other students lived in these districts. Although the differences are not huge, state finance has directed more resources toward districts with large minority enrolllment. For black students, a similar pattern existed under local finance. For Hispanic students, however, the pattern under state finance is a substantive change because, under local finance, those students tended to live in districts with lower revenue per pupil than did other students.

Figures 4.1 and 4.2 focus on revenue per pupil at the district level. This focus has at least two limitations. First, revenues are not resources, and it is the resources provided to students that ought to concern us. Second, resources may be unequally provided across schools within the same district. Betts, Danenberg, and Rueben (2000) address both those limitations by examining the distribution of resources across California schools in 1997–98. Their results are consistent with some findings in this chapter but raise questions about others. When resources are measured by class size, they find very little variation across schools and little correlation with the socioeconomic status of students in those schools. This finding is consistent with our basic results. However, they also find that schools with students of lower socioeconomic status tend to have teachers with less education and experience. This pattern holds across schools in different districts and across schools in the same district. This finding is inconsistent with equality in revenue distributions across income groups, and it suggests an obvious conclusion. Equal revenues for schools may not be sufficient to provide equal resources to schools with large percentages of disadvantaged students.

Conclusion

In 1989–90, the state controlled the allocation of school district revenue. School districts had some sources of local revenue, but those sources constituted only 4 percent of total revenue. The state allocated about 70 percent of total revenue through the system of revenue limits. By design, these funds were distributed very equally. However, the state allocated another 20 percent of total revenue through various categorical programs. Because the state legislature determined the division of funds between revenue limits and categorical aid, and because it determined how categorical aid was allocated, the allocation of total revenues reflected the legislature's preferences.

How did allocations under state finance compare with those under local finance? Under state finance, revenue was more equally distributed across school districts. The remaining differences were mostly due to categorical programs. State finance also improved the relative standing of several large unified districts that had low assessed values and thus low revenues under local finance. They benefited from both the equalization of revenue limits and the allocation of categorical aid. Other large districts tended to maintain their relatively high-spending positions. They had high property wealth under local finance and thus high revenue. Under state finance, the equalization of revenue limits was partly offset by large allocations of categorical aid.

State finance also resulted in a similar distribution of resources across families with different incomes. That result did not represent a real change, however, because revenues were similarly distributed under local finance. The most significant change was for Hispanic students. Under local finance, Hispanic students tended to live in districts with lower revenue per pupil than did other students. Under state finance, however, Hispanic students tended to live in districts with more revenue per pupil than other students. The differences between groups were not large, however.

From the perspective of those promoting more revenue for disadvantaged children, this outcome is disappointing. State finance made redistribution possible, but so far the legislature has not used its authority in any significant way to address the needs of disadvantaged children. As noted long ago by Wise (1967) and Horowitz (1966), equality of revenues among children of different socioeconomic status may still leave disadvantaged children with inferior educational opportunities.

5. Did State Finance Affect Average Spending per Pupil?

As described in Chapter 3, state finance achieved a more equitable distribution of revenues across school districts. It accomplished this by accelerating revenue growth in low-revenue districts and restraining it in high-revenue districts. In choosing which districts to accelerate and which to restrain, the state struck a balance between the cost to taxpayers for public education and the need for additional revenue. Raising all districts to San Francisco's level would have been too costly, but constraining all districts to Garden Grove's level would have been unnecessarily frugal. On balance, taxpayers fared better than schools, as spending per pupil fell in California relative to the national average. This chapter examines possible causes of that decline in spending, including the shift to state finance.

The Decline in Spending per Pupil

As Figure 5.1 indicates, spending per pupil in California between 1969 and 1998 fell about 15 percent relative to the average for the other states. For the decade before the passage of Proposition 13, spending per pupil in California was about 10 percent higher than in the rest of the country. After 1978, spending per pupil grew more slowly in California than in the rest of the country, equaling the level of other states by 1982–83. From 1982 to 1990, spending per pupil in California continued to be about equal to the level in other states. In the 1990s, however, California's average fell below that of other states, reaching a low of 85 percent in 1994–95. It rebounded somewhat after that point, reaching 94 percent of the level of other states in 1997–98.

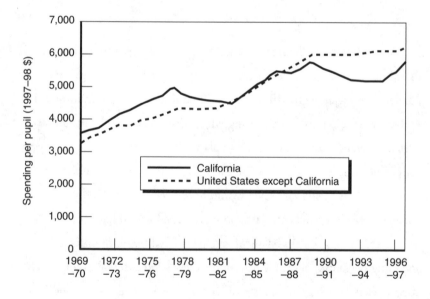

Figure 5.1— Real Spending per Pupil

The measure of spending per pupil used in Figure 5.1 deviates slightly from the measure most commonly used. Usually, spending is the ratio of current expenditures to the number of pupils in average daily attendance. This measure may be misleading for California, however, because of the way the state calculated attendance during this period. In California, students with excused absences were considered to be in attendance—a practice not followed in other states.[1] Consequently, average daily attendance may have overstated the workload of California schools relative to those in other states, thus understating its spending per pupil. An alternative measure to average daily attendance is enrollment—the number of pupils enrolled in a school at a point in time. That measure is used in calculating spending per pupil in Figure 5.1.

Do Economic or Demographic Trends Explain California's Decline?

A state's expenditures on public education may be affected by basic economic and demographic trends, such as income and enrollment growth. Do these basic trends explain California's relative decline in public school spending? In fact, enrollment growth followed a slightly different trend in California than in the rest of the country. In California, enrollments fell from 4.6 million students in 1969–79 to 4 million in 1981–82, then rose to 5.6 million by 1997–98. In the rest of the country, enrollments also fell in the 1970s and rose in the 1980s and 1990s, but the rise was not as rapid as in California. In 1997–98, enrollments in the rest of the United States were still slightly below their

---

[1]Beginning in 1998–99, California no longer counts excused absences as being in attendance.

level in 1969–70, whereas in California, enrollments were more than 20 percent higher in 1997–98 than in 1969–70.

Higher enrollments did not mean that public education was becoming relatively more burdensome to California taxpayers, however. California's population was growing along with its school enrollments. As Figure 5.2 shows, the number of public school students per capita was declining at about the same rate in California as in the rest of the country.

Figure 5.3 shows the burden of public education in a more direct way: real public school spending per capita. From 1969–70 to 1997–98, the burden fell in California relative to the rest of the country. Measured in 1997–98 dollars, California spent about $100 more per capita on its public schools in 1969–70 than did the rest of the country. California's spending per capita fell sharply after Proposition 13; by 1979–80, it was

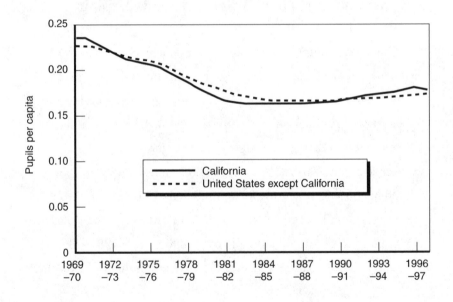

Figure 5.2—Public School Students per Capita

92

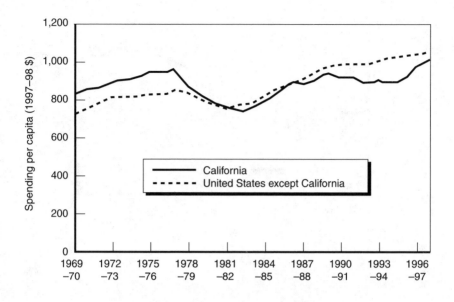

Figure 5.3—Real Public School Spending per Capita

approximately equal to the rest of the country—a level sustained through the 1980s. In the 1990s, California's public school spending per capita fell below that of the rest of the country. By 1993–94, it was more than $100 lower. California's spending per capita recovered somewhat during the last half of the 1990s, but was still lower than the rest of the country in 1997–98.

Although public education did not become more burdensome in per capita terms, it could have become relatively more burdensome to California taxpayers if their incomes had fallen relative to taxpayers in other states. Figure 5.4 compares real personal income per capita in California with that in the rest of the country between 1969 and 1998. By this measure, Californians were better off initially and continued to be better off throughout the period. Because the recession of the early

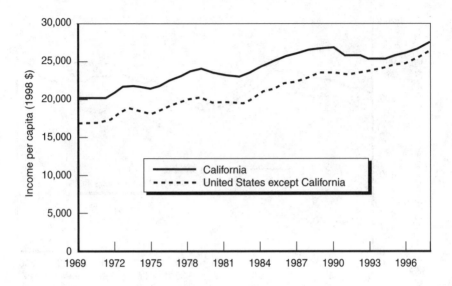

Figure 5.4—Real Personal Income per Capita

1990s was particularly severe in California, there was a narrowing
between it and the rest of the country. Even with this cyclical downturn,
however, California had higher personal income per capita than did the
rest of the United States.

The ability of Californians to finance their schools is also
demonstrated in Figure 5.5, which shows public school spending as a
percentage of personal income. By the standards of the rest of the
country, California could afford to spend more on its public schools in
the 1990s than it actually did. In the early 1970s, California spent about
the same share of its personal income on public education as did the rest
of the country. In the 1990s, California's share was considerably less.

California's growing frugality did not extend to other public services.
As Figure 5.6 shows, California spent more per capita on other public

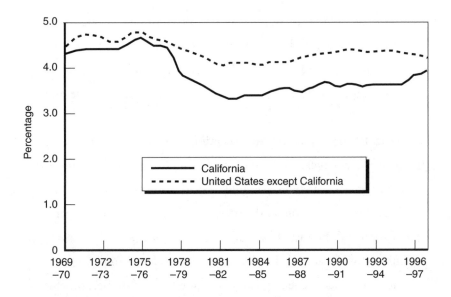

Figure 5.5—Public School Spending as a Percentage of Personal Income

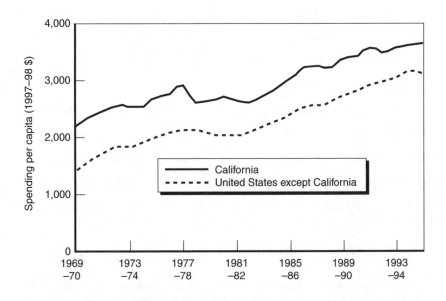

Figure 5.6—Direct, Current Expenditures per Capita by All State and Local
Governments Except Public Schools

services than did the rest of the country. Proposition 13 may have caused a temporary decline in expenditures in the late 1970s and early 1980s, but by the end of 1990s, California was spending about $500 more per capita on other public services than the average for the other states.[2]

The decline in public school spending relative to other spending is particularly remarkable in light of the Gann Initiative, enacted in 1979. That initiative limited the spending of every governmental entity in California to its spending in the previous year adjusted for changes in population and the cost of living.[3] In the case of school districts, population was measured by average daily attendance, implying that no district could increase real spending per pupil. This implication ran directly counter to the *Serrano* mandate. If spending per pupil in the lowest-spending district could not grow any faster than the inflation rate, equalization could be achieved only by limiting all other districts to growth rates in spending per pupil less than the inflation rate. Equalization could be achieved only by reducing real spending in all districts to the level of the lowest-spending district.

Faced with this unpleasant prospect, the state legislature fashioned a compromise. In Senate Bill 1352, the 1980 legislation implementing the Gann Initiative, the legislature excluded from a school district's spending limit all state aid to the district that, when added to its property tax revenue, exceeded its foundation level. This excluded state aid was then

---

[2]Shires, Ellwood, and Sprague (1998) show how revenue sources have changed to mitigate the effects of Proposition 13.

[3]For school districts, the change in the cost of living was the lesser of the change in the Consumer Price Index or the change in California per capita personal income.

included in the expenditures counted against the state's spending limit. Through this device, the state could increase real spending per pupil in low-spending districts by counting that spending against its own limit. If a school district exceeded its spending limit because of the rapid growth in local property tax revenue, the state also allowed that district to count its excess revenue against the state's limit.

In the early 1980s, state tax revenue grew slowly, holding the growth in state spending below the growth in its spending limit. By 1983–84, state spending was substantially below its limit. This trend began to change, however, as the growth in state tax revenues began to accelerate. The Tax Reform Act of 1986 compounded this change because it broadened the base of the federal income tax, which California uses as a base for its own tax, creating a revenue windfall for the state. Ladd (1993) estimated this windfall to be nearly $2 billion per year. In the spring of 1986, the Commission on State Finance estimated that, in 1987–88, the state's revenue would exceed its spending limit by $1.8 billion.[4]

Under the Gann Initiative, the state was to rebate to taxpayers any revenue in excess of its spending limit. The state had an alternative, however. At the time, the State Department of Education estimated that school districts were more than $500 million below their Gann limits.[5] The legislature could have increased the portion of state aid it counted toward school district spending limits, decreased the portion of aid it counted toward the state's limit, rebated less revenue to taxpayers, and

[4]Reinhard (1987).
[5]Reinhard (1987).

increased spending on public schools. It chose not to do so, however, rebating the entire surplus to taxpayers.[6]

This incident fueled the forces behind Proposition 98, the 1988 initiative that placed a constitutional floor on state funds for public schools.[7] The incident also illustrates a fundamental point. California found ways to maintain relatively high spending on public services other than education despite the constraints on that spending. At that same time, it deliberately passed up opportunities to increase funding to public schools. The decline in public school spending in California was a conscious choice.

Explaining the Decline in School Spending

Why did Californians choose to spend less on their schools? Schrag (1998) offers one explanation—an explanation rooted in the growing reluctance of white voters to fund public schools that were becoming increasingly nonwhite. As he points out, "while 46 percent of parents of children under 18 are white, 78 percent of the voting electorate is white."[8] Poterba (1997) finds some support for this explanation in his examination of school spending across states.

There is a different view, however, that is related to California's transformation in school finance.[9] School finance changed the source of

---

[6]Sweeney (1987) describes the legislative debate.

[7]Schrag (1998) describes the campaign for Proposition 98.

[8]Schrag (1998), p. 125.

[9]Silva and Sonstelie (1995) offer another explanation, which is based on an untenable assumption about income homogeneity within districts. Manwaring and Sheffrin (1997) and Downes and Shah (1995) examine whether school finance reform led to a decline in spending in other states.

marginal revenue for public schools—a change that reduced voters' demands for public school spending. A voter's demand for spending on any public service is based on a comparison of perceived benefits and costs. In the case of public education, a voter compares the benefit of increased spending on schools with the higher taxes necessary to finance that spending. To secure higher revenue under local finance, a school district had to levy a higher property tax rate. For homeowners, the higher rate translated directly into higher taxes. For renters, a higher rate may have translated into higher rent, although the connection was certainly less direct. In any event, the school district also levied its tax rate on commercial, industrial, and agricultural property within its boundaries. Revenue from these nonresidential uses of property reduced the revenue required from residential property. In that sense, commercial, industrial, and agricultural property acted as a subsidy to homeowners and renters. It reduced their marginal price of school spending.

The subsidy varied from district to district. On average, nonresidential property accounted for about 45 percent of assessed value in the early 1970s. From 1965–70 through 1972–73, single-family homes averaged 36 percent of the assessed value in the state. Despite the assessment reforms mandated by AB 80 in 1965, the ratio was quite stable during this period, ranging from a low of 34.7 percent in 1967–68 to a high of 37.7 percent in 1972–73. According to the 1970 Census of Population and Housing, single-family homes accounted for about 66 percent of all housing units. Assuming that housing units in multi-unit structures averaged the same assessed value per unit as single-family homes, residential property of all types would have accounted for 55 percent of assessed value. The remainder would have been commercial, industrial, and agricultural property.

Variations in the value of nonresidential property across districts caused variations in assessed value per pupil. Variations in the nonresidential subsidy also caused variations in spending per pupil. The effect of the subsidy on spending is indirectly revealed by the relationship between assessed value and spending, which is demonstrated in Table 5.1. The table separates unified school districts into four groups based on their assessed value per pupil. The four groups are of equal size: each has 59 districts. Assessed value per pupil in the lowest group averaged $6,487 per pupil, and spending averaged $727 per pupil. In the next group, average assessed value was 60 percent higher and average spending per pupil was 6 percent higher. From the second quartile to the third, average assessed value increased by 46 percent, and spending per pupil increased by 11 percent. From the third to the fourth quartile, the increases were 96 percent and 32 percent.

Although these comparisons show that spending is responsive to changes in assessed value, they ignore an important factor. Family

Table 5.1

Assessed Value and Spending per Pupil, by Quartile:
Unified Districts in 1969–70
(in dollars)

Quartile	Average Assessed Value per Pupil	Average Spending per Pupil
First quartile	6,487	727
Second quartile	10,370	770
Third quartile	15,098	854
Fourth quartile	29,566	1,131

income also varied across school districts, and this variation may have confounded the relationship between the nonresidential subsidy and school spending decisions. For example, consider two hypothetical districts, each with the same number of families and students, and each with the same value of nonresidential property. But suppose family income is twice as high in one district as in the other. Families with higher income will tend to live in houses with higher assessed value, so total assessed value in the high-income district will be greater than in the low-income district. Because of the higher residential values in the high-income district, nonresidential property will constitute a smaller fraction of its total assessed value, so its nonresidential subsidy will be lower. In short, higher assessed value per pupil does not always entail a higher subsidy from nonresidential property. A further complication is that, holding constant the nonresidential subsidy, higher-income families will demand more spending per pupil.

Statistical techniques can differentiate between the effects of income on assessed value and its effects on demand. These techniques, which are described in Appendix D, can be used to estimate the elasticity of spending per pupil with respect to assessed value per pupil. The elasticity is the percentage change in spending per pupil resulting from a percentage change in assessed value per pupil. For example, the estimated elasticity is 0.27 for unified districts, meaning that a 10 percent difference in assessed value between two districts with the same median family income was associated on average with a 2.7 percent difference in spending per pupil. For high school districts, the estimated elasticity was 0.26; for elementary school districts, it was 0.17.

Those estimates can be used to address a hypothetical question. Suppose that nonresidential property had been excluded from the property tax base. How would that have affected average spending per pupil in the state? On average, the value of nonresidential property constituted about 45 percent of all assessed value. Removing it from the tax base would have been equivalent to reducing the assessed value per pupil of the average district by 45 percent. According to the elasticity estimates, a 45 percent reduction in assessed value would have reduced spending per pupil by 15 percent in unified and high school districts and by 10 percent in elementary school districts.[10]

This hypothetical exercise is related to the transformation from local to state finance. State finance changed the source of marginal revenue for schools from the property tax to the personal income and sales taxes. Both are direct taxes on families and individuals, with few subsidies from business. In terms of the cost of public schools to voters, moving from local to state finance is similar to removing the nonresidential subsidy under local finance. Removing the nonresidential subsidy under local finance would have decreased demand for spending per pupil by 10 percent to 15 percent. This is approximately the decrease in spending per pupil we actually observed.

Conclusion

From 1970 to 1997, spending per pupil in California fell about 15 percent relative to the rest of the country. This relative decline cannot be attributed to either an increase in the burden of public education or a decrease in personal income. Public education did not become relatively

---

[10]The elasticity estimates are calibrated for small changes in assessed value. Over larger changes, these estimates imply the somewhat larger changes in spending reported in the text.

more burdensome in California. The number of public school pupils per capita fell in California at about the same rate as in the rest of the country. Nor did Californians become relatively poorer; throughout the period, personal income per capita continued to be higher in California. As a percentage of personal income, public school spending fell in California while remaining roughly constant in other states. As further evidence of their disinclination to finance public schools, Californians continued to spend more per capita on other public services than did the rest of the country.

Schrag (1998) argues that California's relative decline in school spending was based on the growing discontinuity between white voters and the growing proportion of nonwhite students. Another explanation is that the transformation from local to state finance increased the marginal cost of public school spending to voters. Under local finance, marginal revenue came from the property tax, and the average voter paid about half the cost of public school spending. Under state finance, marginal revenue came from the sales or personal income tax, and the average voter paid all of the cost. Estimates of voter demand in 1969–70 show that the increase in cost decreased demand for public school spending by 10 percent to 15 percent, which was approximately equal to the relative decline California actually experienced.

6. Did State Finance Affect Class Sizes and Teachers' Salaries?

As a result of the decline in revenues described in Chapter 5, most California school districts had leaner budgets after the switch to state finance. To adjust to their reduced circumstances, districts had several options. They could limit their hiring of teachers, which would increase class sizes. They could also reduce teachers' salaries, although this would hamper their ability to attract and retain the best teachers. A third option was to economize on other expenditures, such as supplies and administrative salaries. In fact, California districts chose mostly to limit their hiring of teachers, causing California's pupil-teacher ratio to rise dramatically relative to that in the rest of the country. California's ratio climbed from 8 percent above the ratio for the rest of the country in 1969–70 to 38 percent by 1996–97. This chapter describes this striking increase and compares California to the rest of the country in teachers' salaries and nonteacher expenditures—the two other areas in which

California school districts might have economized. In doing so, the chapter examines one of the main consequences of school finance reform.

An Accounting Identity

A school district makes many decisions about allocating its resources. This chapter focuses on three basic ones: how many teachers to hire, how much to pay them, and how much to allocate to other expenses. These choices are tied together by the following budget identity:

$$\left(\frac{\text{teachers' salaries}}{\text{current expenditures}}\right) \times \left(\frac{\text{current expenditures}}{\text{pupils}}\right) = \left(\frac{\text{teachers' salaries}}{\text{teachers}}\right) \times \left(\frac{\text{teachers}}{\text{pupils}}\right)$$

The first ratio is the share of the budget allocated to teachers' salaries—a ratio we refer to as the teachers' share. The second ratio is spending per pupil, which is a district's budget expressed in per-pupil terms. The third is average teacher's salary—a measure of the level of teacher compensation. The fourth ratio reflects the workload of teachers. Rearranging terms and using the definitions introduced above, that workload can be expressed directly as

$$\text{Pupils per teacher} = \frac{\text{average teacher's salary}}{\text{teachers' share} \times \text{spending per pupil}}$$

Expressed in this way, the identity shows the basic factors that determine how a district can accommodate a decrease in its budget. If it does not change the average teachers' salary or the teachers' share, it must increase the number of pupils per teacher. To the extent it can either decrease the average salary of teachers or increase the fraction of the budget devoted to teachers' salaries, it can mitigate the increase in average class size. When

allocating their budgets, how did California districts respond to the
reductions after Proposition 13?

Figure 6.1 compares the average teacher's salary in California to the
rest of the country. To adjust for inflation, salaries are expressed in
1997–98 dollars. Between 1969 and 1997, the average teacher's salary
was considerably higher in California than in other states. In 1969–70,
California school districts paid teachers about $8,000 more on average
than did districts in the rest of the country. This difference declined to
$4,700 in 1979–80 but increased throughout the 1980s, reaching $9,000
in 1989–90. It declined steadily from that high, falling to $5,000 by
1996–97.

Figure 6.2 shows the second factor—teachers' share. In California,
that share mirrored changes in that share in the rest of the country.

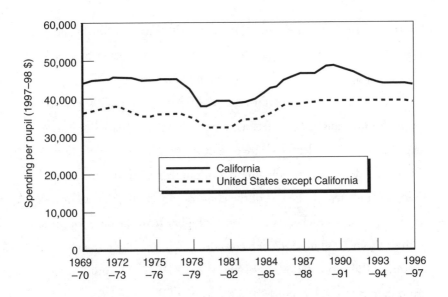

Figure 6.1—Real Average Teacher's Salaries

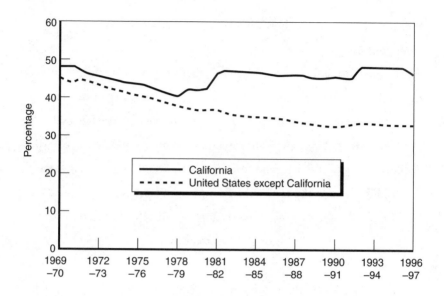

Figure 6.2—Teachers' Salaries as a Percentage of Current Expenditures

Districts throughout the country increased the portion of their budgets allocated to nonteaching expenditures. Despite their leaner budgets, California school districts followed this national trend.

As Figures 6.1 and 6.2 illustrate, California's decline in spending per pupil did not cause a large decline in either teachers' salaries or other expenditures. That left class size to absorb the decline in spending. As Figure 6.3 demonstrates, the number of pupils per teacher rose sharply in California relative to the rest of the country. In 1969–70, California's ratio of pupils to teachers was 8 percent higher than the ratio for other states. From 1969 to 1997, the ratio decreased steadily in the rest of the country. California followed this trend until 1979. The pupil-teacher ratio then rose until it returned to the levels of the early 1970s. In 1996–1997, the pupil-teacher ratio in California was 38 percent higher than in the rest of the country.

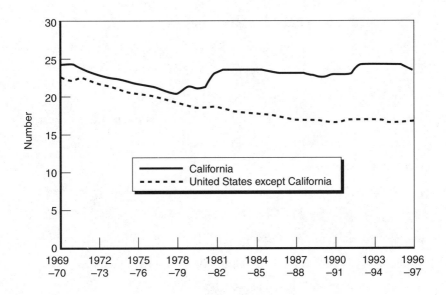

Figure 6.3—Number of Pupils per Teacher

Were California Teachers Paid Too Much?

In reviewing how California school districts adjusted to leaner budgets, one fact stands out. Even as spending per pupil in California fell below that of other states, the average salary of California teachers remained above average. As Peter Schrag wrote, "The power and compensation of teachers have been the granite in the Proposition 13 current; everything else is sandstone."[1] In fact, teachers were not the only granite. As Figure 6.2 shows, California school districts spent an increasing share of their budget on nonteacher expenditures. That share, however, was in line with school districts in the rest of the country, whereas high average salaries for teachers was not. A 1991 study by the

[1]Schrag (1998), p. 78.

Legislative Analyst's Office reached a similar conclusion.[2] It found that increases in K–12 funding in the 1980s had gone mostly to teacher salaries. According to the study, from 1982–83 through 1989–90, the funding for K–12 schools in California rose 13 percent more than would have been required to keep pace with enrollment growth and inflation. None of this increase resulted in a decrease in pupil-teacher ratios; most went to increases in teachers' salaries.

What explains the apparent resilience of teachers' salaries in the face of the general financial decline? One factor may have been the initiation of collective bargaining for teachers, which the legislature authorized in 1976. Schrag suggests another factor that is directly linked to state finance of education.[3] In his view, school districts commanded the interest of the business community when they had the authority to tax. That authority affected the bottom line of local businesses and made them more interested in how their tax dollars were spent. Representatives of the business community served on school boards, bringing their expertise in fiscal management. When school districts lost their authority to tax, they also lost the interest of the business community. School boards had fewer business representatives, strengthening the hand of other interests. Among those other interests were teachers' unions, which became an important force in school board elections. They found candidates sympathetic to their cause, and they supported those candidates with campaign funds.[4]

---

[2]Legislative Analyst's Office (1991).

[3]Schrag (1998), pp. 74–75.

[4]Maureen DiMarco, past president of the California School Boards Association, suggests another factor. Business leaders may have also been less inclined to run for school board positions because of new legislation requiring that candidates for public office disclose their finances.

The centralization of school finance may have strengthened teachers' unions in another way. As the state assumed a larger role in the financing and management of schools, it also affected the bargaining positions of school districts and teachers' unions. As pointed out by the California Commission on Educational Quality,[5] through its legislation affecting such areas as procedures for special education, contributions to the teachers' retirement system, and the length of the school day and year, the state established a base from which collective bargaining began. In that sense, the state legislature mediated the initial round of bargaining between districts and unions—a round that narrowed the scope for further negotiation. This process gave both sides powerful incentives to organize at the state level. Teachers' unions have responded well to these incentives; they constitute the largest source of contributions to Democratic candidates for the state legislature.[6]

The strength of the unions may be an explanation for the high salaries of California teachers. To the extent that state finance has strengthened the hand of the teachers' unions, it is responsible for those salaries and thus for California's relatively high pupil-teacher ratios. But were California teachers really paid too much under state finance? This is not simply a matter of comparing average teacher salaries in California and the rest of the nation. There are other factors to consider, especially the cost of living. During the 1970s and 1980s, housing prices rose rapidly in California relative to the rest of the country. High housing prices increased the cost of living in California and made it more difficult for California school districts to attract teachers from the rest of the

---

[5]California Commission on Educational Quality (1988).

[6]Schrag (1998), p. 75.

country. It also made it more difficult for California districts to retain their teachers.

Several studies have attempted to adjust teachers' salaries for differences in the cost of living across states.[7] These adjustments only raise further questions. Within a city, two houses with identical structural characteristics can have different prices because one has a view and the other does not. In the same way, identical houses in different states can have different prices because of the amenities of the states. A state's amenities include its climate, its terrain, its tax structure, its public services, and a host of other factors.[8] To the extent that housing prices reflect amenities, differences in those prices are not differences in the cost of living. Does the family that chooses to live in a house with a beautiful view have a higher cost of living than a family that chooses to live in an identical house without the view and a consequently lower price?

To ask this question is not to suggest that cost of living is unimportant but only to note that other factors matter as well. In light of these qualifications, the question of whether California districts paid their teachers too much should be rephrased: Given differences in amenities and the cost of living, how much did California school districts have to pay to attract and retain a qualified teaching staff? What salary made them competitive with districts in other states? One way to address these questions is to ask how much other business and government entities in California had to pay to be competitive with

---

[7]See Fournier and Rasmussen (1986), Nelson (1991), and Walden and Newmark (1995).

[8]Roback (1982) and Blomquist, Berger, and Hoehn (1988) examine the effect of amenity differences on wages and housing prices.

similar entities in other states. Their employees experienced the same differences in amenities and costs and had the choice of working in California or in other states. To retain their workforces, California employers had to offer salaries that were competitive with those in other states, given all the nonsalary differences between California and other states.

The salaries of nonteachers are significant for another reason. California school districts compete with districts in other states, but they must also compete with other employers in California. Teachers leave the teaching profession, and workers in other professions become teachers. That fact does not imply that teachers and nonteachers must be paid the same salary; there are amenity differences between teaching and other occupations, and some of these may lead to differences in salary. However, if the salaries of California teachers are too low to compensate for the amenity differences of other occupations, school districts will find it difficult to retain their best teachers.

Location premiums and occupation premiums are relevant in assessing whether California school districts paid their teachers a competitive salary. To be competitive with school districts in other states, California districts may have to pay a location premium. The premium could be negative if California's amenities more than offset its higher cost of living. To be competitive with other employers in California, school districts must also pay an occupation premium, which could be either positive or negative. The location premium is revealed by the difference in pay between nonteachers in California and nonteachers in the rest of the nation. The occupation premium is revealed by the difference in pay between teachers and nonteachers in the rest of the country.

Once determined, these premiums can be applied in two different ways. Consider a hypothetical comparison between teachers' salaries in California and Texas. Suppose that nonteachers in Texas are paid $30,000 a year, teachers in Texas are paid $25,000 a year, and nonteachers in California are paid $40,000 a year. To be competitive, how much must California districts pay teachers? The location premium for California is $10,000—the $40,000 salary of nonteachers in California minus the $30,000 salary of nonteachers in Texas. To be competitive with school districts in Texas, California districts must pay $35,000, which is the $25,000 salary of teachers in Texas plus California's location premium of $10,000. Alternatively, the competitive salary of California teachers can be computed using the occupation premium in Texas. The occupation premium for teaching in Texas is –$5,000—the $25,000 salary of teachers in Texas minus the $30,000 salary of nonteachers in Texas. To maintain the same occupation premium, California districts must pay $35,000, which is $5,000 less than nonteachers earn in California. In effect, the competitive salary of California teachers can be determined by adding the occupation premium to the salary of nonteachers in California or by adding the location premium to the salary of teachers in Texas. Either method yields the same result, a salary for California teachers that is competitive with that of teachers in Texas and also competitive with that of nonteachers in California.

In what follows, we implement the first of these methods, which uses location premiums. Our estimates of these premiums are based on data from the Public Use Microdata Samples of the 1970, 1980, and 1990 Censuses. The datasets are random samples of U.S. households and include extensive information on the incomes and characteristics of household members. From these data, we constructed a sample of adult workers. To make appropriate comparisons with California workers, we restricted the sample to workers from the ten largest states, based on their 1990 population. The ten states cover the major regions of the country. There are three eastern states (New Jersey, New York, and Pennsylvania), three midwestern states (Illinois, Ohio, and Michigan), and three southern states (Florida, North Carolina, and Texas). California is the only western state. To form a group of nonteachers comparable to teachers, the sample was further restricted to full-time workers with at least a bachelor's degree.

The sample had significant variation across states in the average characteristics of workers. Some of these differences may affect average wages. The chief example is age. Age is a good proxy for experience, and experienced workers generally earn more than inexperienced workers, particularly in the case of teachers. Because the average age of teachers differs across states, average wages could also differ, even if states had the same compensation schedule for teachers. We used a standard procedure to account for these differences in characteristics. We estimated the salaries of teachers as a function of their characteristics and then used those estimates to determine the salary a typical teacher would earn in each state. This typical teacher was a person with characteristics equal to the average characteristics over all teachers in our ten-state sample. The procedure is described in more detail in Appendix E.

We used the same procedure to determine location premiums. In this case, we estimated the salary of nonteachers in each state as a function of their characteristics. Using that function, we then determined what a person with the characteristics of the typical teacher would earn as a nonteacher in each state. We refer to this salary as the state's nonteacher salary. The location premium for each state was then calculated as the difference between the state's nonteacher salary and the average of this salary for all ten states. This average was weighted by the number of nonteachers in each state.

The results of these calculations for 1970 are displayed in Table 6.1. After adjusting for differences in characteristics and for location premiums, California teachers averaged about the same salary as for all ten states combined. Without adjustments, the average annual salary of California teachers was $9,570, which was 7 percent higher than the ten-state average. A teacher with average characteristics would have made $9,240 in California, so adjusting for characteristics lowers California's average by $330. The typical teacher would have made $9,107 as a nonteacher in California. The average of this nonteacher salary across all ten states was $8,917, so the location premium for California was $190. After adjustments for characteristics and this premium, the average salary

Table 6.1

Average Annual Salary for Teachers in 1970 in Ten Largest States

State	Average Salary ($)	% of Ten-State Average	$ Adjustments for		Adjusted Salary ($)	% of Ten-State Average
			Charac-teristics	Location Premium		
New York	9,693	109	−114	−600	8,981	101
California	**9,570**	**107**	**−330**	**−190**	**9,053**	**102**
Michigan	9,228	103	306	−517	9,019	101
New Jersey	9,102	102	200	−568	8,737	98
Average	**8,759**	**100**	**39**	**0**	**8,798**	**100**
Illinois	8,606	96	203	166	8,978	101
Pennsylvania	8,410	94	158	513	9,084	102
Ohio	8,149	91	296	308	8,755	98
Florida	7,710	86	261	671	8,645	97
Texas	6,910	77	83	718	7,713	86
N. Carolina	6,881	77	308	1,015	8,206	92

of California teachers was $9,053—2 percent above the ten-state average for adjusted salaries.

Table 6.2 displays the same adjustments for 1980. As in 1970, the adjustments bring California's average closer to the ten-state average. Without adjustments, California's average is 12 percent above the ten-state average. After adjustments, it is 3 percent above. The adjustments account for a large part of the differences in salaries among states. Without adjustments, the range in salaries is very large. North Carolina is 22 percent below the average, and New York is 13 percent above it. With adjustments, the range shrinks from 11 percent below to 4 percent above.

Table 6.3 displays the same information for 1990. The basic conclusion is the same as in 1970 and 1980. The adjusted salary of California teachers is slightly higher than the average for other states. Without adjustments for characteristics and the location premium, the

Table 6.2

Average Annual Salary for Teachers in 1980 in Ten Largest States

State	Average Salary ($)	% of Ten-State Average	$ Adjustments for Charac-teristics	$ Adjustments for Location Premium	Adjusted Salary ($)	% of Ten-State Average
New York	18,462	113	−1,059	−685	16,718	104
California	18,217	112	−1,164	−459	16,595	103
Michigan	18,130	111	−352	−1,220	16,559	103
New Jersey	16,831	103	268	−377	16,722	104
Average	16,338	100	−226	0	16,112	100
Illinois	15,948	98	270	−377	15,842	98
Pennsylvania	15,708	96	145	729	16,583	103
Ohio	14,653	90	409	439	15,500	96
Florida	13,767	84	382	1,704	15,854	98
Texas	13,151	80	630	557	14,339	89
N. Carolina	12,798	78	955	2,005	15,759	98

Table 6.3

Average Annual Salary for Teachers in 1990 in Ten Largest States

State	Average Salary ($)	% of Ten-State Average	$ Adjustments for Charac-teristics	$ Adjustments for Location Premium	Adjusted Salary ($)	% of Ten-State Average
New York	36,607	116	–2,061	–2,469	32,077	102
New Jersey	35,161	111	–742	–3,170	31,249	100
California	34,204	108	–106	–1,949	32,150	103
Michigan	33,797	107	–1,461	114	32,451	104
Average	31,592	100	–287	0	31,305	100
Pennsylvania	30,847	98	–822	2,457	32,482	104
Illinois	29,084	92	–248	972	29,808	95
Ohio	28,775	91	575	1,725	31,074	99
Florida	27,958	88	565	2,529	31,053	99
Texas	25,362	80	1,188	2,445	28,995	93
N. Carolina	24,928	79	1,325	4,576	30,829	98

average salary of California teachers exceeded the ten-state average by 8 percent. With adjustments, California's average is 3 percent above the ten-state average. Across all ten states, the 1990 averages have a smaller range than in either 1970 or 1980. For adjusted salaries, the range is from 7 percent below the average to 4 percent above it—a range of 11 percentage points. In comparison, the range was 16 percentage points in 1970 and 15 points in 1980.

Conclusion

To adjust to leaner budgets under state finance, California school districts had to make difficult decisions. For the most part, they decided to limit their hiring of teachers, causing pupil-teacher ratios to rise dramatically. Alternatively, districts could have limited the growth in teachers' salaries or reduced the portion of their budgets devoted to nonteacher expenditures. Of the two options, teachers' salaries stand out because the average salary of California teachers was considerably above the average in the rest of the nation. Why did California school districts not limit teachers' salaries?

State finance may be partly responsible for this because it lessened the interest of the business community in local school boards and because it centralized some aspects of collective bargaining. Another explanation is that teachers' unions became a powerful force during this period. Yet the purportedly growing influence of the teachers' unions had no measurable effect on teachers' salaries. After adjusting for characteristics and location premiums, the salaries of California teachers were competitive with salaries in other large states. In compensating their teachers, California school districts were responding to market forces. There is little evidence that they paid teachers more than what was necessary to remain competitive. Given those market forces, California school districts could respond to leaner budgets only by increasing class sizes.

7. Did State Finance Affect Student Achievement?

If resources are the only measure, California schools under state finance were inferior to schools in the rest of the country. As Chapters 5 and 6 show, California schools had less revenue per pupil and more pupils per teacher. California schools were also inferior by another measure: student achievement. In the 1992 reading test of the National Assessment of Educational Progress (NAEP), California 4th graders scored the second lowest of 41 participating states. On a scale of 0 to 500, where a "basic" reading level is 212 and a "proficient" one is 243, the average score of public school students was 216 for the United States and 203 for California. The results were similar in the 1994 and 1998 reading tests and the 1992 and 1996 math tests, in which California ranked in the bottom three states. Because these tests were taken well after the state assumed financial responsibility for California's public schools, it is natural to ask whether there was a connection between state finance and the low achievement of California students. This chapter addresses that question.

Possible Connections Between State Finance and Student Achievement

State finance may have influenced student achievement for several reasons. The most direct influence may have been through the level of resources provided to schools. As argued in Chapter 5, state finance caused a relative decline in resources that may have reduced the effectiveness of California's schools. Although this connection seems obvious, it assumes that student achievement is directly related to school resources. In fact, there is a significant body of research questioning that relationship. After reviewing 147 studies, Hanushek (1986) concluded, "There appears to be no strong or systematic relationship between school expenditures and student performance." A related question is whether school resources affect either the earnings or educational attainment of students once they leave school. In reviewing studies of this question, Betts (1996) also finds inconclusive results.

The results of these studies are puzzling. It seems likely that resources matter, at least when properly applied. Perhaps the issue is not the level of resources provided to schools but the incentive schools have to apply those resources effectively. State finance may have affected those incentives in two ways. First, state finance weakened the link between local schools and the population they serve. Under local finance, residents periodically voted on the funding of their schools, imposing a level of accountability. The switch to state finance severed this tie, reducing the accountability of schools. Second, as the state took control

122

of the purse strings, it also began influencing how money could be spent. These attempts interfered with local decisions and diverted resources away from other activities. If the local districts were better attuned to the needs of students, these diversions would have reduced the effectiveness of schools.

An example of the state's growing role was Senate Bill 813, enacted in 1983.[1] The bill had the entirely laudable goal of encouraging districts to devote more of their resources to instruction. It attempted to achieve that goal by giving school districts incentives to allocate money to specific activities. For example, the state distributed an additional $35 per pupil to districts that increased their school year to 180 days. The bill included similar incentives for lengthening the school day and increasing the minimum salary of teachers. Although each of the three actions may be a good use of additional money, all three would not necessarily be the best use of additional money in any one school district. SB 813 did not require that districts undertake any of these actions; it only created incentives for districts and left the ultimate decisions to them. If districts are the best judges of their own needs, however, the money allocated under SB 813 would have been more effectively applied if school districts had received a lump-sum grant and were left to allocate it as they saw fit.

There is some evidence supporting the theory that state finance can undermine the effectiveness of schools. Husted and Kenny (1999) examined the link between the performance of a state's students on the SAT and the degree of state involvement in public school finance. The

---

[1]Picus (1991b) analyzed the effect of SB 813 on school district decisions.

study used two measures of state involvement. The first was the percentage of all public school revenue provided by the state, and the second was the degree of school finance equalization achieved through state policies. Both measures had a negative effect on the average score of a state's students on the SAT. A related group of studies examined the link between statewide tax limitations, such as Proposition 13, and student achievement. Downes, Dye, and McGuire (1998) found only limited evidence that tax limitations in Illinois affect student achievement, whereas Figlio (1997) and Downes and Figlio (1997) concluded that tax limits had a negative effect on student performance.

Do Demographics Explain California's Poor Performance?

Despite the evidence presented by Husted and Kenny, it would be premature to conclude that state finance was a cause of the low achievement of California students in the 1990s. There is at least one other plausible explanation for that poor performance. Compared to other states, California schools had a higher percentage of recent immigrants who were not yet proficient in English. In 1990, about 22 percent of California's residents were foreign-born compared to about 8 percent of residents in the country as a whole. Over 10 percent of the state's population was made up of immigrants who had arrived in the previous ten years—more than three times the national average. Also, 16 percent of California's population did not speak English proficiently, whereas only 6 percent of the country's population fell into that category.[2]

---

[2]*Statistical Abstract of the United States,* selected years.

These demographic differences are reflected in the characteristics of students taking the 1992 NAEP. As Table 7.1 illustrates, California test-takers were more likely to be immigrants or minorities, to have parents with less education, and to speak a language other than English at home. These demographic differences could explain why California's students scored poorly on the NAEP. In fact, these differences account for only part of the poor performance. On the 1992 NAEP reading test, for example, California ranked second to last among participating states and the median California student placed in only the 37th percentile of test-takers in the rest of the country. Using statistical techniques to adjust for demographics differences would move the median California student to the 41st percentile of other states. The state as a whole would still rank in the bottom quartile of the nation.

Although data on individual test-takers are not available for NAEP tests before 1992, they are available for tests taken four years earlier: the

Table 7.1

Characteristics of NAEP Test-Takers
(in percent)

Characteristic	California	United States Except California
Student was born in United States	85	91
White	46	69
Non-Hispanic black	7	17
Hispanic	35	10
Asian	11	2
Father completed high school	42	46
Father completed college	30	27
Mother completed high school	43	51
Mother completed college	27	29
Primary home language is English	42	67

National Education Longitudinal Study (NELS). In addition to providing an opportunity to corroborate the test results from the NAEP, the NELS also allows us to include additional demographic controls to account for the difference in test scores. NELS students completed tests in four subjects: reading, mathematics, science, and history/government. However, one weakness of NELS is that the tests were relatively short. The combined tests lasted only 85 minutes, and the reading test contained only 21 questions and took only 20 minutes. (In contrast, each student in the NAEP reading tests answered 85 questions.) As a result, the NELS scores do not provide precise measurements of student ability. In general, however, the results of the NELS confirm the NAEP results. Students in California performed worse on the exams than students in the rest of the country. The median student in California would place at the 46.5th percentile of test-takers from other states.

Table 7.2 shows the demographic differences between NELS test-takers in California and those in the rest of the nation. As with the NAEP, California test-takers were less likely to speak English at home or to have parents who were high school graduates. Much as in the NAEP, demographic differences can explain about half of the difference between California and the rest of the country. Correcting for the differences in student characteristics increases the scores for California's students but still leaves them below the average scores in the rest of the country. The median student in California would rise to the 48.5th percentile of test-takers from other states.

The NELS test of 1988 and the NAEP test of 1992 paint a similar picture. California students performed worse than students in other states did. Adjusting performance for demographic differences closes some of the gap. It does not close the entire gap, however, leading to the

Table 7.2

Characteristics of NELS Test-Takers
(in percent)

Characteristic	California	United States Except California
White	48	73
Hispanic	28	9
Asian	11	3
Low income	27	28
High income	19	18
Father completed high school	61	68
Father completed college	23	22
Mother completed high school	64	73
Mother completed college	19	18
Primary home language is English	64	85

conclusion that California schools were not as effective as schools in other states during the later half of the 1980s.

Did California Students Perform Better Under Local Finance?

Although California schools may have been less effective than schools in other states in the 1980s, it is still premature to conclude that state finance was the cause. That conclusion requires an affirmative answer to at least one more question. Did California schools actually decline in quality under state finance? Were schools in California comparable to schools in other states before state finance? To address these questions, we turn to two nationally representative tests administered before state finance. The first is the National Longitudinal Study of the High School Class of 1972 (NLS), and the second is High School and Beyond (HSB). HSB was administered in 1980, a little more than a year after state finance was fully implemented because of Proposition 13. The test was administered to 10th and 12th graders, students who received most of their education under local finance. On NLS, California students scored worse than students did in other states: The median student in California would have scored at the 45th percentile for other states. On HSB, California students did better than students in other states; the median Californian placed at the 54th percentile.

Table 7.3 shows the characteristics of test-takers in both exams. In the 1972 NLS exam, California test-takers were quite similar to those in other states. For example, 88 percent of California test-takers spoke English in their homes as compared to 91 percent in all other states. That comparison was considerably different for the 1988 NELS exam, when only 64 percent of California test-takers spoke English at home. In

Table 7.3

Characteristics of HSB and NLS Test-Takers
(in percent)

Characteristic	NLS (1972)		HSB (1980)	
	California	United States Except California	California	United States Except California
White	75	84	72	80
Hispanic	11	3	15	6
Asian	3	1	4	1
Low income	20	22	13	17
High income	23	19	25	20
Father completed high school	72	67	56	55
Father completed college	19	17	23	17
Mother completed high school	72	72	66	65
Mother completed college	11	10	15	12
Primary home language is English	88	91	74	86

1972, the parents of California test-takers were also slightly more educated than those in other states. In the 1988 NELS exam, they were considerably less educated. Although California had a larger share of Hispanic students than the rest of the country in 1972, the difference was not nearly as large as it would become by the time of the NELS and the NAEP.

The similarity in 1972 between California test-takers and other test-takers has a clear implication. Characteristics still have a bearing on the scores of individual test-takers, but they cannot explain the difference between California's schools and those of the rest of the nation. Because the characteristics of students around the country differ much less than they would 20 years later, adjusting test scores for demographic differences scarcely changes California's scores. After adjustments, California's median student would still place at the 45th percentile of students from other states.

For the HSB exam in 1980, the pattern is different. Between 1972 and 1980, the family income of California test-takers increased relative to that in the rest of the country. Not only did California have more high-income families but the state also had fewer low-income families. California also had a larger share of parents who had completed college. Without adjusting for demographics, California test-takers did better than those in the rest of country. However, because the average Californian student with more highly educated parents and higher family income would be expected to score higher than the average student elsewhere, correcting for demographics lowers California's test scores. After the adjustment, California test-takers scored slightly better on average than those in the rest of the country, and the median student in California would place at the 53rd percentile of students in other states.

Taken together, the four exams provide one gauge of how student achievement has changed in California over the past three decades. Under local finance, California test-takers did about as well as those in the rest of the country. Adjusting for characteristics, California students did worse than others in 1972 and a little better in 1980. Under state finance, California test-takers scored worse than students did in other states, especially on the more recent NAEP tests. Adjusting for demographics narrows the gap but does not eliminate it.

Test scores are by no means the only measure of student performance. The HSB and NELS surveys allow a comparison of dropout rates as well because they question students in 10th grade and again in 12th grade. As Table 7.4 shows, California 10th graders were slightly more likely to drop out of school by 12th grade in both 1980 and 1990. This difference persists when we adjust for the differences in demographics. Although students in California dropped out at slightly higher rates than students in the rest of the country, they did so under both state and local finance.

Table 7.4

Dropout Rates of HSB and NELS Students Between
10th and 12th Grade
(in percent)

	California	United States Except California
HSB: 1980–1982	10	8
NELS: 1990–1992	12	10

Do Statewide Exams and SAT Scores Show a Decline in Achievement?

Another source of information on student performance during the past three decades is the series of statewide tests that all students in California take as they progress through school. The California Department of Education has been administering these tests to students for many years, and they may appear to be useful for reviewing the performance of California's students over time. However, the tests suffer from two problems that make comparisons with the rest of the country difficult. One problem is that California periodically changed the test that it used. Between 1970 and 1980 alone, California's 3rd grade students took five different tests. A more serious problem is that it is difficult to compare the results from California to the rest of the nation because different states administer different tests.

No standardized test was given nationwide; to compare students' test scores in California with scores in the rest of the country requires the use of national norms provided by the test publishers. The publishers administer tests to a selected sample of students to determine how scores on different tests are related. In theory, these norms then allow one to compare California's students with students in the rest of the country. However, in practice the norms are not updated very often and may be outdated. Even when timely norms exist, they may not be accurate. Because publishers rely on the cooperation of districts they select to generate the norms, the results become uncertain when some of those districts decline to participate in the norming study. One extreme example taken from a California Department of Education publication illustrates this point. Two reported norms for the test given to 12th graders in the early 1980s differ by so much that one norm would equate a student in California to the nationwide median and another would say that the same student scored at the 33rd percentile.[3]

Although California's statewide tests have limited value for interstate comparisons, SAT scores do not suffer from this disadvantage. Many students across the country take the test each year. The main disadvantage of the SAT is that it does not test a representative sample of the students in the state. The students themselves decide whether to take the test—a fact that has two implications. First, the SAT tests the performance of only a select group of students within a state who are likely bound for college. Even if a state is educating these students very well, it may not be effectively teaching the rest of its student population. The second difficulty with the nonuniversal coverage of the SAT is that the average score for different states probably depends on what percentage of students takes the exam. We could expect higher scores in states where only the best students take the SAT, and lower scores in states where a larger share of the students take the exam.

Even with these weaknesses, the SAT can provide information on the effectiveness of a state's schools. Dynarski and Gleason (1993) demonstrated statistical procedures that produce reasonably accurate state rankings by adjusting SAT scores for the proportion of students who take the exam. We follow their procedure and then compare California's scores to those in the rest of the country.

---

[3]That is not to say that the statewide tests are useless for comparisons within California. Downes (1992) used the statewide tests to examine the effect of revenue equalization on the distribution of student achievement across school districts. He concluded that equalization of revenue did not equalize achievement.

Figure 7.1 illustrates the unadjusted SAT scores for California and the rest of the country during the 1980s and early 1990s.[4] California scored at or above the nationwide average in the early 1980s, roughly tracked the nationwide scores in the mid 1980s, and fell behind in 1993.

As with the other tests, we would expect the characteristics of the students taking the tests to influence the scores. Table 7.5 shows the characteristics of the students who took the SAT between 1980 and 1995. California had a different ethnic mix of test-takers as well as a lower participation rate throughout this time. The lower participation rate should boost scores in California and give the state an advantage in

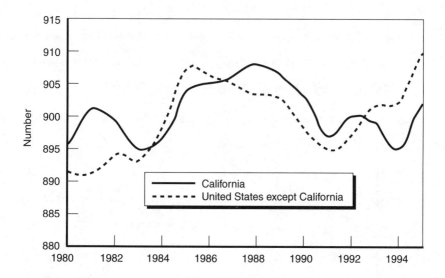

Figure 7.1—SAT Scores

<hr/>

[4]Scores for 1986 were not available and were interpolated from the 1985 and 1987 data.

Table 7.5

Characteristics of Students Taking the SAT
(in percent)

Characteristic	California	United States Except California
Participation rate	45	58
White	57	80
Hispanic	10	2
Black	7	9
Asian	18	4

nationwide comparisons because a more select group of students is taking the exam.

Figure 7.2 illustrates the test scores after they have been corrected for participation rates and demographics. The adjustment generally worsens California's standing. In every year after 1983, students from California

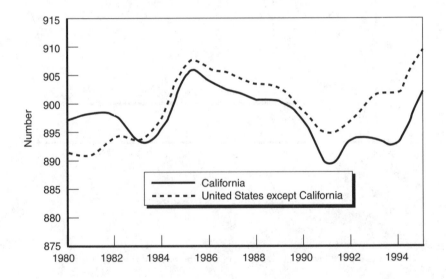

Figure 7.2—Adjusted SAT Scores

score below the rest of the country. California's above-average SAT scores in the late 1980s and early 1990s were caused in large part by low participation rates. These scores corroborate the NELS results and show that Californians were not performing well. Additionally, the SAT scores appear to confirm the evidence from the NAEP that California's performance has been especially poor in more recent years.

How Did State Finance Affect Low-Income Students?

Part of the impetus behind *Serrano v. Priest* was the belief that low-income students were at a disadvantage in California. Although Chapter 2 showed that in 1970 poor families were not segregated into low-spending districts, the changes wrought by state finance may have affected low-income students differently from other students. The test results indicate that California as a whole is suffering compared to the rest of the country, but we have not considered the performance of low-income students. We now use the test scores to analyze the effect of state finance on these students.

The simplest way to examine this issue is to look at the average performance of students by income. Table 7.6 contains the test scores from the NLS, HSB, and NELS by income quartile. There are several ways to interpret these scores. One is to consider the difference in the scores of low-income students between California and the rest of the United States on each of the tests. In 1972, as *Serrano v. Priest* was making its way through the courts, low-income students in California scored 0.8 points better than low-income students in other parts of the country. They improved to 0.9 points better in 1980, but fell 1.1 points behind by 1988.

Table 7.6

Test Scores, by Income Quartile

Quartile	NLS (1972) California	NLS (1972) United States Except California	HSB (1980) California	HSB (1980) United States Except California	NELS (1988) California	NELS (1988) United States Except California
First quartile	46.2	45.4	46.1	45.2	43.7	44.8
Second quartile	48.5	50.1	49.7	49.5	48.0	49.5
Third quartile	50.7	51.9	51.3	50.8	51.9	52.4
Fourth quartile	52.0	54.0	53.4	53.2	55.3	55.1

Alternatively, we can compare the difference in scores of low- and high-income students within California. In 1972, low-income students in California scored 5.8 points worse than their wealthier classmates; in contrast, low-income students in other parts of the country were 8.6 points behind high-income students. In 1980, the gap in California had widened to 7.3 points and in the rest of the country it had narrowed to 8 points. By 1988 low-income students in California fell 11.6 points behind—relatively worse than the 10.3 point gap in other states. Low-income Californians appear to show relatively lower achievement in 1988 than in 1972 and 1980.

Of course, the decline in performance among these students may be caused by demographic changes as more non-English-speaking immigrants moved to California. Following a procedure similar to that outlined above, we can analyze the performance of low-income students in California and adjust for differences in language backgrounds, ethnicity, and parental education. After making these adjustments, we find that low-income students were especially hard hit by the decline in school quality in California (see Appendix F). The median low-income student in California in 1972 would have ranked at the 54th percentile among low-income students in the rest of the country. In 1980, the median California low-income student would have ranked at the 52nd percentile, and by 1988 the median low-income Californian had fallen to the 45th percentile.

Conclusion

Any attempt to use test scores to measure the effectiveness of schools or the effect of policy changes must account for differences in student characteristics. On many of the tests examined in this chapter, demographics explain a substantial portion of the differences in test scores between California and the rest of the country. Simply comparing test scores without adjusting for the types of students tested can provide misleading information. In the tests examined here, the demographic adjustments generally mitigate the apparently lackluster performance of California's schools.

Even after these adjustments, however, some patterns emerge. California's students are now scoring poorly on a range of tests and have been for the past decade. During the 1980s, student performance in California declined even after adjusting for changing student demographics, and the decline may have been worse among low-income students.

The timing of the drop in test scores is suggestive. The group of students in California who participated in HSB and took the SAT in the early 1980s attended school primarily under local finance and scored above the U.S. averages. California's NELS test-takers began school in 1980 under state finance and scored below their counterparts in the rest of the country. By the time of the NAEP tests in the 1990s, California's test scores placed it among the worst states in the country. The decline in scores cannot necessarily be blamed on state finance. It remains the case, however, that student achievement fell soon after California switched to state finance.

8. Did State Finance Cause an Exodus to the Private Sector?

From the perspective of parents in the 1980s and 1990s, conditions in California's public schools must have seemed bleak. In comparison to other states, resources were scarce, classes were large, and students performed poorly on standardized tests. Moreover, the leveling of resources across districts deprived parents of the option to move to a higher-spending district. Schools were underfunded almost everywhere in California, relative to other states, and many of the high-spending schools under local finance experienced the largest cutbacks. If parents were indeed dismayed by their options in the public sector, they had one obvious alternative: They could enroll their children in private schools. Given these conditions, private school enrollment should have mushroomed. Did it? We explore that question in this chapter.

Public School Quality and Private School Enrollment

There is a modest literature on the relationship between public school quality and private school enrollment. Using data from 1970 and controlling for family income and other variables, Sonstelie (1979, 1982) found that private school enrollment was higher in California school districts that had lower spending per pupil. This result suggests that the leveling of school resources caused by *Serrano* and Proposition 13 would increase private school enrollment. Using data from both 1970 and 1980, Downes and Schoeman (1998) examined this prediction. They found that private school enrollment did increase in districts adversely affected by school finance reform. They concluded that reform caused about half the increase in private school enrollment in California between 1970 and 1980. In a recent paper, Evans, Murray, and Schwab (1999) examined whether school finance reform had a similar effect in other states. Although their results are still preliminary, they found that school finance reform did tend to increase private school enrollment nationally.

These papers are careful attempts to sort out the many factors that influence private school enrollment. They focus on the quality of local public schools in a specific district and control for other characteristics of families in those districts. The question we ask is less refined. If parents in California were concerned about conditions in their public schools, and if these schools showed an overall decline relative to other states, private school enrollment should have increased in California relative to other states. We recognize that private school enrollment for the state is an aggregate measure that glosses over conditions in particular school districts. Yet if California's school districts declined generally and significantly in the eyes of parents, that decline should register in the aggregate.

Private school enrollment in California was undoubtedly affected by other factors. For example, examining data from metropolitan areas throughout the nation, Betts and Fairlie (1998) found that private school enrollment increased from 1980 to 1990 in those areas experiencing inflows of immigrant children. California certainly experienced large immigration during this period, suggesting that private school enrollment in the state should have risen as a result of this factor alone.

Figure 8.1 compares private school enrollment in California to all other states. The U.S. data come from the National Center for Education Statistics (NCES), and the California data come from the California Department of Education (CDE). According to these data, the percentage of students in private schools did not increase in California relative to other states. In 1973–74, the earliest year for which the CDE data are available, 8.5 percent of California students were enrolled in private schools as compared to 10.1 percent in the rest of the country. Private school enrollment rose throughout the country during the second half of the 1970s. In California, there was a particularly large increase in 1979 and 1980, immediately after Proposition 13. The proportion of students in private school climbed from 8.8 percent in 1976 to 10.9 percent in 1980, which nearly equaled the percentage in the rest of the country. From that point, however, the proportion of students in private schools increased faster in other states than in California. By 1995, the difference between California and the rest of the country had returned to the 1974 level. In other states, 11.5 percent of K–12 students attended private schools; in California, 9.6 percent attended private schools.

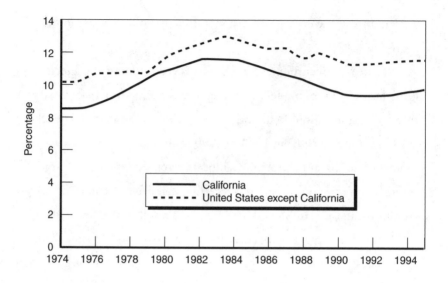

Figure 8.1—Percentage of K–12 Students in Private Schools

A different picture is painted by data from the Census of Population. In states other than California, the proportion of pupils enrolled in private schools fell from 11.7 percent in 1970 to 10 percent in 1990 (see Table 8.1). In contrast, private school enrollments in California rose from 8.5 percent in 1970 to 10.2 percent in 1990. We have more confidence in the Census data than in the data represented in Figure 8.1. The Census counts people the same way in every state, whereas the NCES data rely on state reporting procedures, which may differ from state to state. In fact, for California, the Census and the state procedures give roughly the same answer. According to the data from the CDE, 10.4 percent of California students were in private school in 1980 and 9.9 percent in 1990. From the Census, the comparable numbers are 10.5 percent and 10.2 percent. For states other than California, however, the two sources are further apart. According to the NCES,

Table 8.1

Percentage of Students in Private Schools
in Census of Population

Year	California	United States Except California
1970	8.5	11.7
1980	10.5	10.7
1990	10.2	10.0

10.8 percent of students were in private school in 1980 and 11.9 percent in 1990. For the Census, the comparable figures are 10.7 percent and 10.0 percent. By either source, however, trends in private school enrollment were relatively minor. According to the Census, the private school enrollment rate increased moderately in California while falling somewhat in the rest of the country. According to state reports represented in Figure 8.1, the private school enrollment rate increased slightly in both California and other states.

These aggregate trends may disguise significant changes within subgroups of the population. One subgroup to consider is high-income families. Private schools are expensive, and high-income families are more likely to enroll their children in private schools than are low-income families. Perhaps the poor conditions of California schools caused an exodus of high-income families to the private sector that was not apparent from trends in aggregate enrollment.

To examine that issue, we use data on families with school-age children from the Censuses of 1970, 1980, and 1990. For each year, families were assigned to deciles based on their annual income measured in 1990 dollars. Table 8.2 shows the maximum income for each decile.

Table 8.2

Maximum Annual Income for Family Income Deciles
in Families with School-Age Children
(in 1990 dollars)

Decile	1970	1980	1990
First decile	13,474	10,802	9,933
Second decile	20,885	17,717	17,200
Third decile	26,948	23,808	23,900
Fourth decile	31,328	29,439	30,000
Fifth decile	35,707	34,594	35,925
Sixth decile	40,423	39,670	42,084
Seventh decile	46,486	46,015	50,000
Eighth decile	54,234	53,945	60,000
Ninth decile	68,045	68,213	78,000

For example, the second decile in 1970 consisted of families with income greater than $13,474 but less than or equal to $20,885.

The decile boundaries reveal an increase in income inequality between 1970 and 1990. The boundary between the ninth and tenth deciles was nearly $10,000 higher in 1990 than in 1970, whereas the boundary between the first and second decile was about $3,500 lower in 1990 than in 1970. This pattern is consistent with the findings of Reed, Haber, and Mameesh (1996), which show that income inequality increased throughout the country during this period and was particularly evident in California.

Table 8.3 shows private school enrollment in each income decile. As the table demonstrates, the increase in California's private school enrollment has come mainly from higher-income families. Among children from families in the 8th income decile in 1970, 10.1 percent went to private school in California as compared to 14.8 percent in the rest of the country. In both 1980 and 1990, however, this percentage

Table 8.3

Percentage of School Children Enrolled in Private Schools,
by Family Income Decile

Decile	1970		1980		1990	
	California	United States Except California	California	United States Except California	California	United States Except California
First decile	3.9	4.8	5.6	5.4	3.9	3.6
Second decile	4.3	6.0	6.6	6.3	3.8	5.1
Third decile	4.8	7.7	7.3	7.9	5.1	6.5
Fourth decile	5.8	10.3	7.8	9.2	6.3	8.3
Fifth decile	8.5	11.8	9.1	10.2	9.2	9.0
Sixth decile	9.2	12.9	10.6	10.8	8.5	9.6
Seventh decile	9.5	13.5	10.6	11.4	10.3	10.7
Eighth decile	10.1	14.8	13.7	12.8	13.5	12.4
Ninth decile	10.4	16.0	12.8	14.0	14.5	14.4
Tenth decile	14.1	20.9	17.2	19.9	20.8	21.4

was higher in California than in the rest of the nation. A similar pattern holds for the top two deciles. In 1970, a considerably lower percentage of California students from these deciles were enrolled in private schools compared to the rest of the country. By 1990, the percentage was nearly the same.

Conclusion

By most objective measures, the overall conditions of California schools worsened under state finance. Spending per pupil fell relative to other states, the pupil-teacher ratio rose, and California students began to perform worse than other students on standardized tests. School finance reform also reduced the range of choices in the public sector because it equalized revenue across districts. If these worsening conditions concerned parents, private school enrollment in California should have increased noticeably.

Private school enrollment did increase somewhat, particularly among high-income families. But even among these families, it did not exceed the rate in the rest of the country. We conclude that, although California parents had ample reason to be discouraged about their public schools, their discouragement was not great enough to cause a significant exodus to the private sector.

9. Have Voluntary Contributions Undone Equalization?

As the previous chapter demonstrated, the poor conditions of California schools under state finance did not engender a dramatic increase in private school enrollment. However, it did provoke another response: Parents began to voluntarily contribute to their local public schools. Following school finance reform in California, many school districts established educational foundations designed to channel private contributions into public schools. Before 1971, fewer than ten of these organizations operated in California. There are now more than 500. Furthermore, PTAs and booster clubs in recent years have become much more active in fund-raising activities. How large are the contributions raised by these organizations, and have they undermined the state's attempts to equalize resources across districts? In this chapter we explore these questions by documenting the size and distribution of voluntary contributions to California's public schools.

Identifying Voluntary Contributions

Contributions to California's public schools are channeled through nonprofit organizations with tax-exempt status. We have obtained data on these contributions from the income statements these organizations file with the Internal Revenue Service and with the Registry of Charitable Trusts (RCT) of the California Attorney General's Office. At the school level, most contributions are raised by PTAs, PTOs (Parent Teacher Organizations), and booster clubs. At the district level, contributions are raised primarily by local educational foundations. These organizations are required to file an RCT Form CT-2 if their income exceeds $25,000 in a year. Each organization's income is publicly available on the RCT Master File.

PTAs are an exception to this practice. Because of the large number of these organizations in California, the RCT requires only the 36 regional offices of the California PTA to report. However, individual PTAs are required to file an IRS Form 990 if their average yearly income exceeds $25,000. The income statements of these organizations are publicly available on the IRS Master Business File. Using these state and federal nonprofit tax return records, we have attempted to identify the revenue raised by all nonprofit organizations supporting K–12 public schools. A detailed description of the method used to identify these nonprofit organizations can be found in Brunner and Sonstelie (1996).

In many respects, local educational foundations are the most interesting type of nonprofit organizations supporting California's public schools. Unlike PTAs and booster clubs, which have been supporting public schools for years, most educational foundations were established only after school finance reform began in California. Figure 9.1 shows the number of educational foundations operating in California by year of

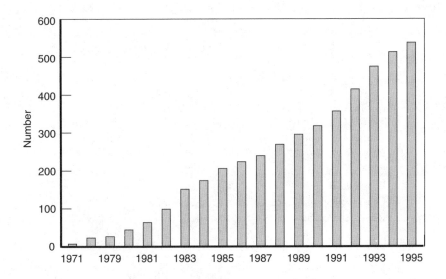

Figure 9.1—Number of Local Educational Foundations in California

establishment. Before 1971, the year of the *Serrano* decision, there were
six educational foundations in the state; in 1978, the year in which
Proposition 13 was passed, there were only 22. In the two years
immediately following Proposition 13, however, the number of
educational foundations more than doubled to 46. Since 1980, the
number of foundations has grown steadily. Between 1980 and 1994, an
average of 32 new foundations have emerged annually. Currently, there
are more than 500 educational foundations in operation.

The Size of Voluntary Contributions

Table 9.1 documents the total revenue raised by nonprofit
organizations supporting public schools in California during the 1994
tax year. The first column subdivides nonprofit organizations into six
general categories. The category Other local organizations includes

Table 9.1

Total Revenue of K–12 Nonprofit Organizations
in the 1994 Tax Year

Type of Organization	No. with Gross Revenue of $25,000 or More	Total Revenue ($)
Educational foundations	282	55,692,610
PTAs	885	81,532,162
PTOs	190	30,116,671
Booster clubs	284	40,694,724
Other local organizations	52	6,607,592
Urban foundations	7	11,776,938
Total	1,700	226,420,697

organizations such as school alumni associations and school bingo clubs. The category urban foundations includes educational foundations that support large urban school districts such as Los Angeles Unified. Whereas local educational foundations rely heavily on individual donations, urban foundations tend to rely primarily on donations from large corporations.

For each type of organization, Column 2 of Table 9.1 lists the total number of organizations that filed with either the RCT or the IRS during the 1994 tax year. Column 3 gives the total revenue raised by each type of organization. As the totals indicate, these organizations raised over $226 million for California's public schools during the 1994 tax year.

Table 9.1 reports gross revenue, but a better measure of support may be net revenue, defined as gross revenue less total operating costs. The IRS Master Business File does not include net revenue figures, but the RCT Master File contains them for a subset of the organizations that report each year. The net revenue figures were available for approximately 11 percent of the nonprofit organizations in our sample. Using those net revenue figures, we calculated that net revenue was approximately 65 percent of gross revenue. That percentage implies that nonprofit organizations raised approximately $146 million in net revenue, or $28 per student, for California's public schools in 1994. Although the number is small, it is growing rapidly. Brunner and Sonstelie (1996) reported that in 1992, nonprofit organizations raised approximately $97 million in net revenue, or $19 per student, for California's pubic schools. Thus, between 1992 and 1994, voluntary contributions to California's public school grew by approximately 50 percent.

Table 9.2 documents the average revenue per pupil raised by K–12 nonprofit organizations in 1994. The first row lists the average revenue per pupil raised by organizations associated with a specific elementary or middle school. Similarly, the second row states the average revenue per pupil raised by organizations associated with a specific junior or senior

Table 9.2

Revenue, by School or District Type in the 1994 Tax Year

	No. of Schools or Districts	No. with Revenue of $25,000 or More	Average Revenue per Pupil ($)	No. with Revenue per Pupil of $100 or More	Average Revenue per Pupil ($)
School level					
Elementary school	5,719	1,035	202	511	345
High school	1,405	326	125	83	262
District level					
Elementary school	591	70	258	30	566
Unified	304	100	47	10	314
High school	106	21	11	0	0

high school. The last three rows show the average revenue per pupil raised by organizations associated with either an elementary school, unified, or high school district.[1] For example, of the 5,719 elementary and middle schools in California, 1,035 (18 percent) had a nonprofit organization that raised over $25,000. Among these 1,035 schools, revenue per pupil averaged $202. Similarly, of the 591 elementary school districts in California, 70 had a nonprofit organization that raised over $25,000. Among these 70 districts, revenue per pupil averaged $258. The fourth column lists the number of schools or school districts that had a nonprofit organization raising over $100 per pupil, and the fifth column shows the average revenue raised by those organizations. For example, 511 of the elementary and middle schools (8 percent) had a nonprofit organization that raised over $100 per pupil. Among these 511 schools, revenue per pupil averaged $345. Similarly, 30 elementary school districts had a nonprofit organization that raised over $100 per pupil. Among these school districts, revenue per pupil averaged $566.

The Distribution of Voluntary Contributions

The revenue figures reported in Tables 9.1 and 9.2 highlight several interesting facts. First, contributions per pupil are quite small for the state as a whole. If the $226 million raised in support of California's public schools were distributed equally across all districts, it would amount to about $43 per pupil. Second, although contributions per pupil tend to be small on average, several schools and school districts have been quite successful in raising private contributions. For example,

---

[1]Of the 1,001 school districts in California, 296 have just one school. We included the contributions made to these single-school districts in the district-level figures.

contributions per pupil exceeded $100 in more than 500 of the elementary and middle schools in California. This second fact raises the question: Which schools have been most successful in raising voluntary contributions? In this section we explore that question by documenting the distribution of voluntary contributions to California's public schools.

We begin by examining the relationship between voluntary contributions and the constraints imposed on district resources by revenue limits. Recall that revenue limits were the primary tool used by the state to equalize resources across districts. Districts with high revenue limits in 1974–75 had their limits leveled down over time whereas districts with low revenue limits in 1974–75 had their limits leveled up over time. Thus, if voluntary contributions have been used to offset the equalizing effects of revenue limits, contributions should be highest among those districts with high revenue limits in 1974–75.

Table 9.3 provides evidence consistent with that hypothesis. It provides information on school-level and district-level contributions per pupil for elementary school districts, separated into quartiles by 1974–75 district revenue limits.[2] The first quartile corresponds to districts with the lowest revenue limits in 1974–75; these are the districts least constrained by reform. The fourth quartile corresponds to districts with the highest revenue limits in 1974–75; these are the districts most constrained by reform.

---

[2]Because of the formation of new school districts or the consolidation of existing districts, 1974–75 revenue limits were unavailable for ten of the 591 elementary school districts operating in California in 1994–95. Of the 63 schools located in these ten school districts, six had a nonprofit that raised over $25,000. Among these six schools, the average contribution per pupil was $198. Furthermore, six of the ten school districts had a district-level nonprofit that raised more than $25,000. Among these six districts the average contribution per pupil was $51.

Table 9.3

Contributions per Pupil, by Quartiles of 1974–75 Revenue Limits: Elementary School Districts

Quartile ($)	School-Level Contributions[a]		District-Level Contributions[a]	
	% with Revenue of $25,000 or More	Average Revenue per Pupil ($)	% with Revenue of $25,000 or More	Average Revenue per Pupil ($)
First quartile 0–762	12	102	5	68
Second quartile 763–832	11	160	10	231
Third quartile 833–1,066	20	144	10	112
Fourth quartile 1,067 and above	37	390	21	418

[a]1994 tax year.

Schools located in districts that were most constrained by reform were the most successful in raising voluntary contributions. Of the 233 schools located in districts with revenue limits of $1,067 or more in 1974–75, 37 percent had a nonprofit that raised over $25,000. Among these schools, the average contribution per pupil was $390. In contrast, only 12 percent of the 269 schools located in districts with revenue limits of $763 or less had a nonprofit that raised over $25,000. Among these schools, the average contribution per pupil was $102. A similar pattern holds for district-level donations. For example, of the 144 districts with a revenue limit of less than $763, only seven had a nonprofit that raised over $25,000. In these districts, the average contribution per pupil was $68. In contrast, 30 of the 146 districts with a revenue limit of $1,067 had a nonprofit that raised over $25,000, and their average contribution per pupil was $418.

Table 9.4 shows that a similar relationship between contributions per pupil and 1974–75 revenue limits holds for unified school districts.[3] Schools located in districts that were most constrained by reform were the most successful in raising voluntary contributions. Twenty-one percent of the schools located in districts with a 1974–75 revenue limit of $1,121 or more had a nonprofit that raised over $25,000. Among these schools, the average contribution per pupil in 1994 was $267. In contrast, of the 1,068 schools located in districts with a 1974–75 revenue limit of $890 or less, 17 percent had a nonprofit that raised over $25,000. Among these schools, the average contribution per pupil was

Table 9.4

**Contributions per Pupil, by Quartiles of 1974–75 Revenue Limits:
Unified School Districts**

	School-Level Contributions[a]		District-Level Contributions[a]	
Quartile ($)	% with Revenue of $25,000 or More	Average Revenue per Pupil ($)	% with Revenue of $25,000 or More	Average Revenue per Pupil ($)
First quartile 0–889	17	146	22	8
Second quartile 890–944	17	136	31	17
Third quartile 945–1,120	19	205	51	52
Fourth quartile 1,121 and above	21	267	35	100

[a]1994 tax year.

---

[3]1974–75 revenue limits were unavailable for 38 of the 304 unified school districts operating in California in 1994–95. Of the 317 schools located in these 38 school districts, 58 had a nonprofit that raised over $25,000. Among these 58 schools, the average contribution per pupil was $178. Furthermore, eight of the 38 school districts had a district-level nonprofit that raised over $25,000. Among these eight districts, the average contribution per pupil was $18.

$146. Appendix Table H.1 contains the same table for high school districts. As that table illustrates, school-level and district-level contributions per pupil tended to be much smaller in high school districts. Furthermore, there is no consistent relationship between 1974–75 revenue limits and contributions per pupil for school-level donations.

The figures reported in Tables 9.3 and 9.4 are consistent with the hypothesis that voluntary contributions have been used to offset the equalizing effect of revenue limits. Contributions per pupil are largest among those schools and school districts that were most constrained by the revenue limit system. Although revenue limits are the most obvious measure of the severity of the constraints imposed by school finance reform, they may not be the best one. By using 1974–75 revenue limits to measure how constrained districts are in 1994–95, we are essentially assuming that the demand for spending per pupil within districts has not changed over time. In other words, we are assuming that high-spending districts in 1974–75 would be high-spending districts two decades later if they were not constrained by the revenue limit system. There are two reasons not to make this assumption. First, the demographics of districts have changed. Numerous studies have shown that the demand for spending per pupil is positively related to the income of families in a district.[4] Thus, changes in family income in those two decades could have changed the demand for spending per pupil. Second, as we showed in Chapter 5, the levels of spending per pupil that existed in the 1970s reflected the marginal prices of school spending that districts faced in those days. Districts with a high percentage of commercial and industrial

---

[4]See, for example, Borcherding and Deacon (1972), Bergstrom and Goodman (1973), and Bergstrom, Rubinfeld, and Shapiro (1982).

property faced low marginal prices and therefore chose relatively high revenue per pupil. Because state finance eliminated the subsidy, 1974–75 revenue limits may overstate the demand for spending per pupil. These facts suggest that family income may better measure the severity of constraints imposed by reform. If wealthier families have greater demands for school spending, contributions per pupil should be highest among those schools and school districts whose residents have the highest family income.

Figure 9.2 provides evidence consistent with that hypothesis. It illustrates the relationship between 1990 family income and school-level contributions per pupil in 1994. The vertical axis measures contributions per pupil for the elementary and middle schools with contributions of $25,000 or more. For each school, the horizontal axis

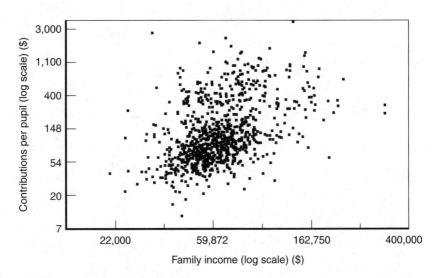

Figure 9.2—Family Income (1990) and School-Level Contributions per Pupil (1994)

gives the average income of families in the school's census tract.[5] As hypothesized, contributions per pupil appear to be positively related to family income.

Figure 9.3 illustrates the relationship between family income and district-level contributions per pupil.[6] As with school-level contributions per pupil, district-level contributions per pupil appear to be positively related to family income.

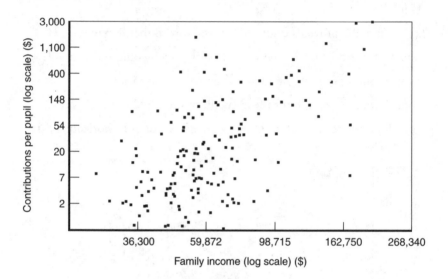

Figure 9.3—Family Income (1990) and District-Level Contributions per Pupil (1994)

---

[5]We were unable to obtain family income data for 408 of the elementary and middle schools operating in California in 1994–95 (see Appendix H for more details). Of these 408 schools, 33 had a nonprofit that raised over $25,000. Among those 33 schools, the average contribution per pupil was $185.

[6]1990 district-level family income data were unavailable for 222 of the 1,001 school districts operating in California in 1994–95 (see Appendix H for more details). Of these 222 districts, 25 had a nonprofit that raised over $25,000 and five had a nonprofit that raised over $100 per pupil. All five school districts that raised over $100 per pupil were located in the relatively affluent counties of Santa Barbara and Monterey.

Table 9.5 documents the relationship between family income and contributions per pupil in more detail. In schools with an average family income of $29,999 or less, only 1.4 percent had a nonprofit that raised over $25,000 in 1994. Among these ten schools, revenue per pupil averaged only $60. In contrast, 58 percent of schools with an average family income of $100,000 or more had a nonprofit that raised over $25,000 in 1994. Among these 105 schools, revenue per pupil averaged $427. For each range of family income, the third column gives the percentage of schools with a nonprofit organization that raised over $100 per pupil in 1994, and the fourth column gives the average revenue raised by these organizations. Only 0.3 percent of the schools with an average family income of $29,999 or less raised over $100 per pupil. In contrast, 51.1 percent of the schools with an average family income of $100,000 or more raised over $100 per pupil in 1994. Among these schools, revenue per pupil averaged nearly $500. The same information for junior and senior high schools is given in Appendix H.

Table 9.5

Family Income and School-Level Contributions[a] per Pupil: Elementary and Middle School Districts

1990 Average Family Income ($)	% with Revenue of $25,000 or More	Average Revenue per Pupil ($)	% with Revenue per Pupil of $100 or More	Average Revenue per Pupil ($)
0–29,999	1.4	60	0.3	182
30,000–49,999	8.3	135	2.5	324
50,000–69,999	30.0	150	12.0	271
70,000–99,999	52.0	260	34.4	358
100,000 and above	58.0	427	51.1	475

[a]1994 tax year.

Table 9.6 documents the relationship between district-level contributions per pupil and family income. As the table illustrates, districts with the highest family income were the most successful in raising voluntary contributions. Of the 83 districts with an average family income of $29,999 or less, only 2 percent had a nonprofit organization that raised over $25,000 in 1994. Furthermore, none of the districts with an average family income of $29,999 or less had a nonprofit organization that raised over $100 per pupil. In contrast, of the 29 districts with an average family income of $100,000 or more, 72 percent had a nonprofit organization that raised over $25,000 and 55 percent had a nonprofit organization that raised over $100 per pupil. In these 16 districts, average revenue per pupil exceeded $700.

Table 9.6

Family Income and District-Level Contributions[a] per Pupil: All School Districts

1990 Average Family Income ($)	% with Revenue of $25,000 or More	Average Revenue per Pupil ($)	% with Revenue per Pupil of $100 or More	Average Revenue per Pupil ($)
0–29,999	2	130	0	—
30,000–49,999	11	22	0.2	410
50,000–69,999	32	99	6	445
70,000–99,999	55	69	11	223
100,000 and above	72	548	55	708

[a]1994 tax year.

Voluntary Contributions and Revenue Equalization

As we have seen, some schools and school districts have been quite successful at raising voluntary contributions, particularly those most constrained by reform. Yet the question remains: Have voluntary contributions undone equalization? Table 9.7 provides an answer to

Table 9.7

Distribution of Students, by Ranges of Contributions per Pupil

Contribution ($)	School-Level Contributions (%)	District-Level Contributions (%)
0–0.99	78.0	54.0
1–49.99	7.3	41.0
50–99.99	6.7	3.6
100–199.99	4.3	0.6
200–499.99	2.4	0.6
500 and above	1.3	0.2

that question by listing the proportion of students who benefited from the different levels of voluntary support. For example, 78 percent of all students attended a school in which school-level contributions per pupil were less than one dollar. Similarly, 54 percent of all students attended a district in which district-level contributions per pupil were less than one dollar. The numbers reported in Table 9.7 suggest that voluntary contributions have not undone equalization. Rather, an overwhelming majority of students attended a school or school district in which contributions per pupil were quite small. Specifically, 92 percent of all students attended a school in which contributions per pupil were less than $100, and only 1.3 percent of all students attended a school with contributions per pupil of $500 or more. Similarly, 98.6 percent of all students attended a district in which contributions per pupil were less than $100, and only 0.2 percent attended a district with contributions per pupil of $500 or more.

Conclusion

By the early 1990s, many school districts were left with less revenue than they would have had under local finance. Many turned to voluntary contributions from parents and others. Following school finance reform, the number of educational foundations operating in California grew dramatically. Furthermore, PTAs, PTOs, and booster clubs became much more active in fund-raising in recent years. In 1994, nonprofit organizations such as these raised over $226 million in voluntary contributions for California's public schools.

Although $226 million represents a substantial sum, it nevertheless amounts to only about $45 per pupil. Of course, voluntary contributions are not equally distributed across schools and school districts. In some, particularly those most constrained by reform, contributions per pupil are quite large. Have those contributions undone equalization? In terms of the percentage of students that attend a school or are in a school district that raised substantial contributions, the answer is clearly no. Over 90 percent of all students attended a school or were in a school district in which contributions per pupil were less than $100 per year. Even in those very few cases in which contributions per pupil were as much as $500, contributions were only about 10 percent of total revenue.

10. Has State Finance Equalized Quality?

By 1990, the transformation from local to state finance was complete. Although school districts had independent sources of discretionary revenue, including voluntary contributions and other local revenue not subject to the revenue limit, these sources constituted a relatively small portion of total revenue. For most practical purposes, the state controlled the allocation of school district resources. Has the state used this control to ensure that every district offers the same quality of education to its students? Although school quality is difficult to assess, one way to measure the judgments and attitudes of parents concerning the quality of schools is the amount they are willing to pay for houses in specific school districts. If state finance has equalized quality, families would not be willing to pay large housing price premiums to live in one school district rather than another. This chapter examines those premiums for districts in Los Angeles and Orange Counties.

Public School Quality and Housing Values

One measure of school quality is student achievement on standardized tests. In an important paper, Downes (1992) attempted to determine whether the transformation from local to state finance resulted in an equalization of student achievement. To do so, he used school district averages on the standardized tests given as part of the California Assessment Program. Comparing results in 1976–77 with results in 1985–86, Downes concluded that there was no evidence of equalization in student achievement. Judging by that evidence, state finance did not appear to equalize quality.

Although this evidence is important and compelling, it is not a complete answer to the question we pose. Student achievement is certainly an important element of any measure of school quality, but it is not the only one. Parents weigh other factors as well, including the richness of a school's curriculum; the variety of its extra-curricular programs in the arts, music, and athletics; the competence of its career and college counselors; the conditions of its buildings and grounds; and the quality of its special education program. All of these elements count in different ways for different families.

With enough information about each of these elements, it would be possible to calculate an index of school quality similar to the rankings of the quality of life in different cities. As in the case of city rankings, however, the values of this index may be revealed by the actions of individual decisionmakers. This point was first made in a seminal paper by Tiebout (1956). Tiebout observed that families shop for communities much as they shop for any other good. In a metropolitan area, they typically have many communities in which they could choose to live, and each offers a different bundle of public services and other amenities. For families with children, the most important publicly provided service is public education. Real estate agents respond to parental concerns about public school quality by providing prospective homebuyers with information about the schools or school districts in different communities. Similarly, metropolitan newspapers often publish the test scores of students enrolled in different schools and school districts.

If families respond to this information in the manner suggested by Tiebout, the price of a house should reflect not only its physical characteristics and those of the surrounding neighborhood but also the quality of public education provided by the school district in which it is located. In other words, there should be a premium attached to the prices of homes located in good school districts because families are willing to pay more for them. This premium is a measure of public school quality as perceived by parents.

Measuring Public School Premiums

How much are parents willing to pay for a home located in a good school district? As Bogart and Cromwell (1997) note, in an ideal setting we could answer that question by comparing two homes that are identical in every relevant respect except for the school districts in which they are located. The homes would have the same physical characteristics, the same property tax payments, and the same neighborhood characteristics; the only difference between them is the school district in which they were located. In that case, any difference in the price of the two homes could be attributed to the difference in the quality of the two districts. Of course, homes located in different districts are rarely identical. They differ in structural characteristics, property tax payments, and the characteristics of the neighborhoods surrounding them. The separate effects of all of these characteristics, including school district quality, can be identified through statistical techniques.[1]   One of the earliest and most influential studies examining the effect of public school quality on housing values was conducted by Oates (1969).   Using a sample of 53 northern New Jersey communities, he examined the relationship between housing values and inter-jurisdictional differences in public school quality and tax rates. As a proxy for public school quality, Oates used spending per pupil. After controlling for neighborhood characteristics, tax rates, and the structural characteristics of homes in different communities, he found that homes located in communities with higher spending per pupil had higher housing values.

Since the pioneering work of Oates, a host of studies have examined the relationship between housing values and public school quality using samples drawn from different metropolitan areas and alternative measures of public school quality.[2]   In general, these studies have found that houses located in districts of higher quality have higher values, all else equal. In a study of a 1970 sample of houses in San Mateo County, Reinhard (1981) found that houses located in school districts with higher student performance on standardized tests or higher spending per pupil had higher housing values. Specifically, each additional month of

---

[1]For a more detailed discussion of these issues, see Rosen (1974) and Freeman (1979).

[2]See, for example, Li and Brown (1980), Jud and Watts (1981), Haurin and Brasington (1996), and Black (1997). Also see Crone (1998) and Fischel (1998) for excellent reviews of the literature on housing values and public school quality.

average reading improvement achieved by students in a school district increased the sale price of a home by $1,468, and each additional dollar of per pupil expenditures increased the sale price of a home by approximately $27.[3]

To put these numbers in context, consider a home selling for $30,000, which approximates the median sale price of homes in Reinhard's sample. Furthermore, suppose this home was located in a school district with spending per pupil of $950, which approximates the median level of spending per pupil among school districts located in San Mateo in 1970. Now consider a similar home located in a school district with spending per pupil of $1,285, which corresponds to the 95th percentile of spending per pupil among school districts in San Mateo in 1970. All else equal, the sale price of this home would have been $39,045 or approximately 30 percent higher than the home located in the district with spending per pupil of $950.

Reinhard's results suggest that differences in public school quality played an important role in explaining housing values before school finance reform in California. Specifically, families were willing to pay large housing price premiums to live in good school districts. Did the transformation from local to state finance cause those premiums to disappear?

School Districts in the Los Angeles Metropolitan Area

Our analysis used data from Los Angeles and Orange Counties. We selected this area because it contains a large number of diverse school

---

[3]Sonstelie and Portney (1980) obtained similar results using the same data.

districts from which families may choose. In 1990, 1.67 million students were enrolled in 99 school districts located within this region. Of these 99 school districts, 36 were elementary school districts, 9 were high school districts, and 54 were unified school districts. We excluded a number of these school districts for several reasons. Because the boundaries of elementary and high school districts overlap (several elementary school districts are typically associated with one high school district), we eliminated high school districts from our sample. We also eliminated 12 districts because a recent annexation or consolidation prevented us from accurately identifying their boundaries.[4] Our final sample contains 48 unified school districts and 29 elementary school districts.

The size and socioeconomic composition of the 77 school districts in our sample varied widely. In 1990, these districts contained 951,000 families and 1.44 million students, which represented 86.2 percent of all students located within the region. The largest school district, Los Angeles Unified, enrolled more than 595,000 students whereas the smallest school district, Hermosa Beach Elementary, enrolled only 722 students. Family income also varied widely across districts. In the five wealthiest districts, average family income in 1990 exceeded $138,000; in the five poorest districts, it was below $33,000.

---

[4]The 12 districts that were eliminated from the sample are Las Virgenes Unified, Hacienda-La Puente Unified, Placentia Unified, Saddleback Valley Unified, Los Alamitos Unified, Capistrano Unified, Alhambra City Elementary, Lowell Joint Elementary, Manhattan Beach City Elementary, Redondo Beach City Elementary, San Gabriel Elementary, and Soledad-Agua Dulce Union Elementary.

The Housing Sample

Our data on house prices come from the Experian Company, formerly TRW. Each observation is the record of a specific sale of an owner-occupied single family home that sold during 1990 in one of the 77 school districts included in our sample. There are 41,852 observations. The Experian database includes every piece of property in California. It is continually updated and, for every property, contains the address and other locational information, a detailed list of physical attributes, and information on the two most recent sales. The data are generally available to appraisers and real estate agents on a fee-for-use basis. Variables describing the physical characteristics of each home include both quantity and quality measures. House size is described by square footage of living space, number of bathrooms, and lot size or land area. House quality is described by the age of the house and the number of fireplaces. Quality is also described by whether the house has a view, whether it has a pool, and whether it has central air conditioning.

We matched each home in our sample with six measures of neighborhood quality. Three variables describe the Census tract in which the house is located; these are the percentage of the population age 65 or older, the percentage below the poverty level, and time to work. All three were constructed using tract-level data from the 1990 *Census of Population and Housing*. In addition to the Census tract variables, we used three other neighborhood indicators: environmental quality, which is measured by the annual average air pollution readings for total suspended particulates; crime rate, measured at the city level as the FBI index of major crimes; and neighborhood accessibility to the beach, calculated as miles to the nearest beach.[5]

Table 10.1 lists the variables used in our analysis. The average sale price of homes in our sample was $255,962. However, this average value masks considerable variation across districts in housing values. For example, the average sale price of a home exceeded $600,000 in five school districts. In contrast, the average sale price of a home fell below $150,000 in four districts. Of course, these gross differences in housing

Table 10.1

Measures of Structural and Neighborhood Characteristics

	Mean
Structural characteristics	
No. of bathrooms	1.78
Presence of central air conditioning (yes=1, no=0)	0.19
No. of fireplaces	0.60
Age of home	41.51
Lot area in square feet	7,999
Interior living space in square feet	1,549
Presence of pool (yes=1, no=0)	0.18
Presence of a view (yes=1, no=0)	0.03
Neighborhood characteristics	
% in Census tract above 65 years old	11.79
Miles to nearest beach	17.14
% in Census tract below poverty level	10.68
Per capita FBI crime index	77.14
Time to work in minutes	28.33
Annual average of total suspended particulates (parts per million)	94.09
Sale price, $	255,962

[5]Variables that depict neighborhood/community influences are matched to the housing data using common location indicators. For most variables the matching exercise is straightforward because a home is located within a specific Census tract and city. However, the air pollution data require a multi-step procedure to assign a specific Census tract the appropriate pollution measures. We assign air pollution to each location using the method developed by Beron et al. (1998) in their recent report to the South Coast Air Quality Management District.

values result from many factors other than public school quality. For example, homes located in the five districts with the highest average sale prices tended to be much larger than homes located in the four districts with the lowest average sale prices. To identify the effect school district quality has on housing values, we sought to separate it from the effect of other structual and neighborhood characteristics that vary systematically across school districts.

School District Housing Price Premiums

Our estimation procedure is a simple one. We estimated the price of a house as a function of its structural characteristics, its neighborhood characteristics, and the school district in which it was located. Using that estimate, we then determined the premium for each school district. The premium is the percentage increase in the price of a house resulting solely from its school district. This premium is measured relative to houses in Los Angeles Unified. Thus, a premium of 10 percent for a particular school district means that, all else equal, houses in that district have a price that is 10 percent higher than houses in Los Angeles Unified.

The premiums for ten representative school districts are presented in Table 10.2. A complete listing of all 76 is presented in Appendix Table I.1. There is substantial variation in these premiums. To provide some context for the magnitude of these premiums, the average school district premium in our sample was 10 percent. Thus, relative to Los Angeles Unified, location within the average school district adds 10 percent to the value of a home, all else equal. Across the entire sample, the estimated premiums range from –24 percent to +45 percent. Ten school districts in our sample have housing price premiums of 30 percent or

Table 10.2

School District Housing Price Premiums

	Premium (%)
La Canada Unified	40
Hermosa Beach City Elementary	27
Monrovia Unified	23
Duarte Unified	17
Pomona Unified	10
Orange Unified	8
ABC Unified	5
Westminster Elementary	2
Garden Grove Unified	−3
Long Beach Unified	−9

[a]Percentage premium relative to Los Angeles Unified School District.

higher, and eight school districts have premiums of minus 10 percent or lower.

These premiums translate into substantial differences in housing prices. To illustrate that point, consider two identical homes, one in Duarte Unified and the other in Monrovia Unified. Duarte Unified and Monrovia Unified border each other on the eastern edge of the Los Angeles metropolitan area. The two districts are roughly the same size; in 1990, Monrovia Unified had an enrollment of 5,253 and Duarte Unified had an enrollment of 4,383. They also contained families with similar socioeconomic characteristics. Despite these similarities, we estimate that homeowners are willing to pay 6 percent more to live in Monrovia Unified rather than Duarte Unified. For the average house in the two districts, the 6 percent premium means that the home located in Monrovia Unified is valued at approximately $15,350 more.

For the homebuyer, this premium is a one-time payment for the right to live in Monrovia Unified instead of Duarte Unified. When the buyer sells the house at some future time, the payment can be recovered, provided the housing price differential continues to exist. Even if it is recovered, however, the buyer pays a price for residing in Monrovia instead of Duarte. For each year of residence, the buyer pays additional property taxes and additional mortgage interest, payments that are not recovered when the house is sold. The additional property tax is $154, the 1 percent property tax rate multiplied by $15,350; and the additional mortgage interest is $1,535, the 10 percent mortgage interest rate that prevailed in 1990 multiplied by $15,350. Thus, for the average house, the price of living in Monrovia Unified instead of Duarte Unified is $1,689 per year.

This price reflects differences between the two districts in the quality of schools as perceived by homebuyers. It may also reflect other differences between the two areas that are not identified in the statistical analysis we perform. These other differences may include differences in the quality of other public services and differences in the quality of the housing stock not captured in our analysis. As a consequence, our results are more suggestive than definitive. Differences in school district quality are undoubtedly a contributing factor to the large housing price premiums reported in Tables 10.2 and Appendix Table I.1, but there may be other factors as well.

Conclusion

The 1974 ruling of the Los Angeles Superior Court established the parameters for school finance reform in California. Differences between school districts in assessed value per pupil could not lead to substantial differences in revenue per pupil. However, differences in the educational needs of students were a legitimate reason for differences in revenue. The state responded to this mandate by creating the revenue limit system to offset differences in property tax revenue. It also created a host of categorical programs to address the special needs of school districts and their students. Under this system, the state had the authority to allocate revenue among districts in whatever manner it found appropriate.

Did the state use this authority to ensure that every school district offered an education of the same quality? If quality is measured by housing premiums associated with particular school districts, the answer is no. Large premiums suggest that homebuyers perceive large differences in the quality of school districts. Although we cannot attribute all of these premiums to school district quality, it is surely an important factor.

11. Has State Finance Been Good for California?

In the last five years, four major reports on school finance in California have appeared. All have recommended a return to local finance. The first report was from Policy Analysis for California Education (PACE), a consortium of education researchers at Stanford University and the University of California, Berkeley. Its 1995 report concluded that local communities "have lost control of their schools because they have lost control of the dollars."[1] As a remedy, PACE recommended a constitutional amendment authorizing school districts to levy a property, parcel, or income tax with a simple majority vote.

Constitutional change was precisely the mandate of the California Constitution Revision Commission, which the governor and the legislature created to examine the structure of state government. In its 1996 report, the commission noted that the centralization of school

---

[1]Policy Analysis for California Education (1995), p. 13.

finance has "fostered a disconnect between citizens and their local education system."[2] To reconnect citizens with their schools, the commission recommended that school districts use two methods to raise their own revenue. Under the first method, with a two-thirds vote of their residents, school districts would increase the property tax rate above the Proposition 13 limit. Under the second method, a simple majority of county voters would approve a half-cent increase in the sales tax, with the proceeds allocated to districts on a per pupil basis.

The third report was published in July 1997 by the bipartisan Little Hoover Commission, which was created in 1962 to promote efficiency in state government. Noting that the school finance system was unnecessarily convoluted, it characterized the system as one in which "Money reaches districts, school campuses and individual classrooms through complex formulas that are difficult to understand and that are constantly manipulated by state policy makers, state bureaucrats, school administrators and outside consultants." Following the suggestions of John Mockler and Bill Whiteneck, two respected experts on California's school finance system, the commission recommended a simpler method of allocating state revenue based on student counts weighted by a small number of factors. It also recommended "Re-enforcing local control of schools by creating a local funding option."[3]

The Legislative Analyst, Elizabeth Hill, released the fourth report in May 1999. It called for a process that would sort out the proper roles of state and local governments in the finance and governance of California's public schools. After an extensive review of the research on public school

---

[2]California Constitutional Revision Commission (1996), p. 49.
[3]Little Hoover Commission (1997), p. 6.

governance, the report identified local flexibility as a critical ingredient for successful schools. Arguing that this flexibility is often reduced by state regulations, the report recommended a return to a "locally oriented governance model." It concluded that this return is unlikely to occur unless school districts have the authority to raise their own tax revenue. The Analyst cited two reasons for this conclusion, both of which are worth quoting in their entirety.

> First, even if the Legislature gives substantial flexibility and autonomy to school districts, that freedom will not generate the breadth or intensity of interest in district affairs on the part of voters and businesses compared to district proposals for changed tax rates. As a consequence, the lack of local revenue discretion threatens the development of strong local accountability.

> Second, with no additional local revenue discretion, the powers of the state and local districts would not be balanced. Instead, the state would remain the dominant power and the sole source of funding for most districts. In addition, without strong local accountability, the state would likely take a stronger role in regulating district practices. Thus, over time, the state probably would "reregulate" K–12 education.[4]

Although the recommendations of these four reports vary in their details and their rationales, all share the view that state finance has not been good for California. Does the evidence support that view?

A Summary of the Evidence

We found that state finance has resulted in a more equal distribution of revenues across districts. There are still inequities, but they pale in comparison to the inequities under local finance. Although this considerable achievement should not be overlooked or understated, it is mitigated by the nature of the inequities the reformers sought to address.

---

[4]Hill (1999), p. 53.

These inequities were based primarily on differences in assessed value across districts and were not correlated with family income. Certainly, some districts had many wealthy families and high spending per pupil, but there were also high-spending districts with many low-income families. We found considerable variation in revenue per pupil within income groups but similar distributions across those groups. Local finance may not have been equitable, but it did not discriminate against low-income families.

In the face of these inequities, the courts ruled that differences in property wealth across districts must not lead to significant differences in district revenue—a requirement the state has satisfied through its revenue limit system. However, the courts also held that categorical aid, which the state allocates to districts according to their special needs, did not have to be distributed equally across districts. Because the state can determine where and how much of its revenue to distribute as categorical aid, it has had considerable latitude in allocating revenue among districts. As Chapter 4 showed, however, it has used this latitude conservatively. The state has not directed significantly more revenue to districts with large numbers of disadvantaged students. From the perspective of reformers, the distribution of revenues under state finance has been disappointing.

Whereas the courts have focused primarily on the distribution of revenues across districts, school districts and parents have been more concerned with the level of resources provided to schools. According to this measure, state finance has not been successful. Between 1970 and 1998, spending per pupil in California fell more than 15 percent relative to spending in other states. We explain this decline by noting the effects of state finance on the demand for school spending. Under local finance, nonresidential property taxes subsidized the residents' demand for school spending. State finance, however, ended this subsidy and thereby curbed this demand.

School districts absorbed the decline in spending by increasing class sizes. By 1997, the pupil-teacher ratio in California was 38 percent higher than the ratio in other states. The decline in spending did not appear to affects teachers' salaries. Some have hypothesized that state finance increased the power of the teachers' unions, which then used their strength to protect salaries during lean times. Our findings indicate that school districts were responding more to market forces than to union power.

Revenues, class sizes, and teachers' salaries are inputs to the educational process. The output is the education of students. By that measure, California schools have not fared well under state finance. Using data from four different achievement tests between 1972 and 1992, and correcting for demographic differences between California and the rest of nation, we found that California students were on par with students in the rest of the country during the first half of this period but fell behind during the second half. Results from the SAT paint a similar picture. Under state finance, student achievement fell.

Achievement tests are one way to measure the quality of a school. A more important measure, perhaps, is the way parents responded to their perceptions of public school quality. Private school enrollments increased among high-income families, and a few wealthy communities contributed significant time and money to their local schools. Parents also paid housing price premiums to live in districts with good schools. We found a range of such premiums among school districts in Los

Angeles and Orange Counties. The large ones suggest that parents in those counties do not perceive equal quality across school districts.

After reviewing this evidence, it is difficult to argue that state finance has been good for California. It has equalized revenues across school districts, but it has not directed more resources to disadvantaged students or equalized quality across districts. Furthermore, state finance has equalized revenue by leveling down, decreasing average spending per pupil and increasing the state's pupil-teacher ratio relative to other states. Although state finance is not necessarily to blame for poor performances on achievement tests, it remains true that these performances have gotten worse under state finance. Increases in private school enrollment and voluntary contributions to public schools also suggest that California parents are increasingly dissatisfied with public education.

An Institutional Framework for State Finance

Because the courts forced California policymakers to focus on the distribution of resources, it is not surprising that less attention has been paid to ensuring that those resources have been used effectively. Nor is it surprising that the four most recent major reports have focused on weaknesses in public school governance. California has changed the way it finances its public schools without changing the way it governs them. From this perspective, state finance cannot yet be judged a failure. Until school governance conforms to the structure of public school finance, it will not have had a fair trial.

What institutional changes would be necessary to give state finance a fair trial? We do not pretend to have a complete answer to that question, although some problems with the existing institutions are apparent. One problem is the uneven balance of political power among school districts.

Every school district has its own special needs for additional revenue. Under state finance, the legislature decides which needs can be funded and which cannot. Large districts are at an advantage in this process because they have more representatives in the legislature and can afford to hire lobbyists. Consequently, the legislature is more likely to understand and respond to the needs of these larger districts. The legislature seems more likely to allocate resources efficiently if districts are approximately the same size. In his presentation to the Little Hoover Commission, Bill Whiteneck suggested a model for that reorganization. Under the Whiteneck model, all districts would be unified districts with approximately 15,000 to 20,000 students. Each would have three or fewer high schools and the elementary schools feeding those high schools.[5] Under that model, California would have about 300 school districts, each equivalent in size and political power.

Although the Whiteneck model has clear advantages over the current structure, it raises an even more fundamental question. Why have school districts at all? School districts are the primary taxing authority under local finance, and it is therefore natural to give them the primary authority to govern schools. Placing governing authority at the same location as taxing authority promotes accountability and prudent fiscal decisionmaking—a theme common to the four reports reviewed above. Applying the same principle to state finance, however, implies that the state should have the primary authority to govern schools. It also implies that school districts and elected school boards have no role to play.

Under the current arrangement, the state exercises its authority through regulations and legislation, which are blunt administrative

---

[5]Little Hoover Commission (1997).

instruments. Imagine, in contrast, a system of public schools in which each school is essentially an office of the California Department of Education and each employee in the system is ultimately accountable to the Superintendent of Public Instruction. Regional offices would serve some of the functions of school districts, but the lines of authority would be more clearly drawn, and funds could be allocated to school sites more flexibly. It would be easier to establish consequences for poor performance and rewards for good performance. It would also be easier to hold teachers, principals, and school sites accountable to state guidelines. In short, a centralized school system would replace legislative rulemaking with bureaucratic control.

Another way to implement state finance with less bureaucracy is through charter schools, which were authorized by Senate Bill 1448 in 1992. Charter schools are exempt from most state regulations and operate according to the goals and procedures spelled out in their charter petitions. The governing board of a school district approves these petitions and assumes oversight responsibility for the school. In many cases, charter schools were public schools that petitioned their own district's board to become chartered. However, a school could petition any district. In theory, at least, a district could charter a school situated within the boundaries of another district. In that case, state revenue would follow the students. Under SB 1448, operating funds for the charter school are funneled through the school district approving the charter.

According to Wells (1998), the amounts of these funds have often been negotiated between the charter school and the district. In practice, this could mean that charter schools would receive less money than their enrollments actually generate. These financial arrangements are being changed as a result of Assembly Bill 544, passed in 1998. Charter schools now receive block grants based on per pupil revenue that a typical school district would receive from revenue limit and categorical funds. AB 544 also authorized County Offices of Education and the State Board of Education to issue up to 100 new charters each year.

Under the new funding model, charter schools will have more autonomy. The model will deliver a level of funding to charter schools equivalent to that of most public schools, and it will deliver those funds without strings attached. The funds will come as a direct block grant based only on the number and grade level of students enrolled in the school.[6] Some observers have raised concerns about the accountability of charter schools, which receive substantial public funds without the oversight that governments usually provide.[7] Although these concerns may prove to be valid, they seem to miss an important point. Under the charter school model, parents bear the ultimate responsibility for educating their children. They have a choice between enrolling their children in a charter school or in the local public school. As long as parents exercise those choices intelligently, charter schools are held accountable. A charter school that fails to offer an education of comparable quality to the local public school will have no students, and thus no resources. In this sense, charter schools combine some of the best aspects of state finance and local control. The schools will receive state revenues but have the freedom to adapt to local needs.

---

[6]The model also allocates extra funds for students with limited English proficiency and for students eligible for the free or reduced-price lunch program.

[7]For example, see Hall and Goldfinger (1999).

With the new funding model, we believe that many more public schools will petition to become chartered. As that happens, however, we can also foresee a time in which the state may come under more pressure to regulate charter schools, which brings us back to the fundamental point made by the Legislative Analyst. Is it possible for a public school to be truly local without its own revenue source?

A Return to Local Finance

If the answer to that question is no, as the Legislative Analyst argues, and local control is as important as the recent reports contend, then the state should give school districts the authority to raise their own local revenue. This conclusion immediately raises the question of whether California can return to local finance and still satisfy the courts. Our reading of the *Serrano* decision suggests that it can. The courts focused on differences in revenue across districts that were due to differences in property wealth. The implication is that, if differences in property wealth could be effectively neutralized, differences in revenue per pupil are tolerable. District power-equalization, as originally proposed by the *Serrano* plaintiffs, satisfies that requirement. Under that scheme, the same tax rate produces the same revenue per pupil, regardless of the district's tax base. In effect, the state guarantees that every district has the same tax base. It does this by providing the difference between what the district would raise if its chosen tax rate were applied to the guaranteed base and what the district actually raises by applying that tax rate to its own base.

District power-equalization achieves a form of horizontal equity, or the like treatment of equals. It also has elements of vertical equity insofar as it favors districts with low family income. With district power-equalization, the same property tax rate leads to the same revenue per pupil. Lower-income families will tend to live in houses with lower assessed value and thus will pay lower taxes for a given level of revenue per pupil.

In one sense, Proposition 13 may have made it easier to implement district power-equalization, whose biggest hurdle is "recapturing" tax revenue in high-wealth districts. Recapture occurs when the assessed value per pupil in a district is higher than the state's guaranteed tax base. In that case, district property owners end up paying more in additional property taxes than their district receives in revenue. The difference is recaptured by the state and used to subsidize lower-wealth districts, a very unpopular idea in an era when each district viewed its property tax revenue as its own. That era disappeared in California with the passage of Proposition 13. Under the current system, any increase in property tax revenue in a district is captured entirely by the state, because it reduces, dollar for dollar, the state aid that must be allocated to the district.[8] From this new status quo, additional revenue to the district is more like a gift bestowed by the state than the state theft of local property tax revenue.

Proposition 13 may also be the biggest stumbling block to local finance. The property tax is the most natural local tax because it is administered locally, it taxes an immobile source, and it funds local services whose benefits are capitalized back into that source. Yet because Proposition 13 expressly forbids an increase in the property tax above 1 percent, a constitutional amendment would be required to remove that limit. Parcel taxes are another possibility. School districts already have

---

[8]The exception is the small number of basic aid districts.

the right to levy it, and it can be administered using the same structure as the property tax. If the use of parcel taxes became widespread, however, a *Serrano*-type suit would surely challenge its constitutionality. In that case, the state would have to design a power-equalization scheme to offset differences in parcels per pupil across districts.

Another revenue option for school districts is the local income tax. Because the tax is not applied at the local level in California, this option is often dismissed as administratively unfeasible. It is not, however, as Ohio's experience with a school district income tax demonstrates.[9] As with the property tax or the parcel tax, a power-equalization scheme could easily be devised to offset differences in personal income across districts.

A final hurdle to all local revenue options is Proposition 218, which passed in 1996. Under its provisions, school districts must secure the approval of two-thirds of their voters to enact a new tax. Although many regard the two-thirds hurdle as too high, the measure does not prevent school districts from raising local revenue.

In summary, there are serious obstacles to the full implementation of state governance and equally serious obstacles to a return to local finance. As a result, California seems stuck in the middle, which may be the worst of all worlds.

---

[9]See Payton and Hack (1995).

Appendix A

Data Sources for Material in Chapter 2

Assessed Value, Tax Rates, Enrollment, and Revenue Sources

These data are from *Annual Report of Financial Transactions Concerning School Districts of California: Fiscal Year 1969–70,* which is published by the California State Controller. There were 1,337 districts in the report, 1,080 of which reported having positive enrollment. In the 1969–70 fiscal year, six unified districts had junior colleges: Glendale, Long Beach, Santa Monica, Palo Verde, San Diego, and San Francisco. By the next fiscal year, the junior colleges in all of these districts had separated from the unified districts and had formed distinct community college districts. For these six districts, enrollment and revenue data from 1970–71 were substituted for 1969–70 data. The revenue data were deflated by the increase from 1969–70 to 1970–71 in total revenue per pupil for all California schools. The deflation factor was 95.7 percent.

In Figures 2.3, 2.5, 2.6, 2.7, and Table 2.2, property taxes are district taxes plus tax relief subventions from the Controller's report. State aid is school fund apportionments plus other state revenue from the Controller's report. Federal aid is total federal plus total combined federal and state from the Controller's report. Other local revenue is total county plus sales and rentals plus other local revenue from the Controller's report.

Family Income

These data are from the "1970 Census Fourth Count: School District Data Tapes." The Census reported data on 740 of the 1,080 districts listed in the Controller's report. The total enrollment of the 340 districts that were excluded from the Census data was 78,407, which is 1.7 percent of the total number of public school students in California. All but five of the districts not included in the Census had enrollment less than 500 students. The five districts larger than 500 students (the largest had 17,000 students) were all involved in consolidations between 1969 and 1971.

In Figures 2.10 and 2.11, the family income groups are aggregates of the 15 groups in Census Table 75.

Student Race and Ethnicity

These data are from the *California State Testing Program: 1970–71 Profiles of School District Performance*, published by the California State Department of Education.

Supplementary Tables for Chapter 2

The sources of district revenue, depicted for unified districts in Figure 2.3, are listed for all districts in Table A.1.

The distribution of total revenue per pupil, depicted in Figure 2.9, is listed for all districts in Table A.2.

Table A.1

Revenue per Pupil in 1969–70
(in dollars)

Revenue Source	Elementary School Districts	High School Districts	Unified Districts
Property taxes	373	623	478
State aid	300	266	276
Federal aid	42	42	48
Other local revenue	13	21	15
Total revenue	728	952	817
No. of districts	723	120	236
No. of students	1,137,471	538,527	2,938,622
Average enrollment	1,573	4,488	12,452
Median enrollment	364	1,716	4,406

Table A.2

Distribution of Revenue per Pupil in 1969–70
(in dollars)

	Percentile[a]				
Revenue Source	5	25	50	75	95
Elementary school districts					
Property taxes	179	253	321	442	718
Property taxes + state aid	516	597	635	718	932
Total	582	645	693	775	1,003
High school districts					
Property taxes	287	423	610	696	1,081
Property taxes + state aid	671	798	856	954	1,235
Total	739	859	924	1,014	1,305
Unified districts					
Property taxes	225	360	469	538	845
Property taxes + state aid	614	684	747	778	1,010
Total	669	733	818	839	1,138

[a]Weighted by district enrollment.

The distribution by family income of total revenue per pupil, depicted in Figure 2.11 for unified districts, is given for all districts in Tables A.3, A.4, A.5, and A.6.

Table A.3

Distribution of Total Revenue per Pupil, by Family Income Group: Unified Districts in 1969–70
(in dollars)

| | Percentile[a] | | | | |
Income	5	25	50	75	95
0–2,999	682	761	839	847	1,449
3,000–5,999	674	753	839	840	1,374
6,000–7,999	671	753	839	840	1,449
8,000–9,999	668	747	829	839	1,374
10,000–11,999	665	745	824	839	1,374
12,000–14,999	665	750	827	839	1,374
15,000–24,999	668	753	839	848	1,374
25,000 and over	689	782	839	868	1,449

[a]Weighted by families.

Table A.4

Distribution of Total Revenue per Pupil, by Family Income: Elementary School Districts in 1969–70
(in dollars)

| | Percentile[a] | | | | |
Income	5	25	50	75	95
0–2,999	580	648	698	782	1,011
3,000–5,999	578	648	698	782	1,011
6,000–7,999	582	648	698	782	1,016
8,000–9,999	586	649	698	782	1,016
10,000–11,999	600	649	702	782	1,011
12,000–14,999	600	651	702	793	1,016
15,000–24,999	603	659	712	817	1,065
25,000 and over	600	678	734	897	1,125

[a]Weighted by families.

Table A.5

Distribution of Total Revenue per Pupil, by Family Income:
High School Districts in 1969–70
(in dollars)

Income	Percentile[a]				
	5	25	50	75	95
0–2,999	752	886	932	1,018	1,305
3,000–5,999	752	886	932	1,018	1,305
6,000–7,999	752	886	932	1,019	1,305
8,000–9,999	752	884	932	1,025	1,305
10,000–11,999	752	886	932	1,035	1,305
12,000–14,999	752	886	932	1,037	1,305
15,000–24,999	752	886	939	1,037	1,305
25,000 and over	752	910	966	1,097	1,334

[a]Weighted by families.

Table A.6

Distribution of Total Revenue per Pupil, by Family Income:
Unified Districts Except Los Angeles in 1969–70
(in dollars)

Income	Percentile[a]				
	5	25	50	75	95
0–2,999	668	733	805	912	1,449
3,000–5,999	666	733	792	891	1,449
6,000–7,999	666	733	792	891	1,449
8,000–9,999	643	730	784	868	1,449
10,000–11,999	643	730	784	868	1,449
12,000–14,999	643	730	784	868	1,449
15,000–24,999	643	733	802	890	1,449
25,000 and over	675	753	827	946	1,449

[a]Weighted by families.

The distribution of total revenue per pupil by race and ethnicity, depicted in Figure 2.13 for unified districts, is given in Tables A.7, A.8, and A.9 for all districts.

Table A.7

Distribution of Total Revenue per Pupil, by Race and Ethnicity:
Unified Districts in 1969–70
(in dollars)

Race/Ethnicity	Percentile[a]				
	5	25	50	75	95
Black	729	839	839	946	1,089
Hispanic	643	733	805	839	990
All	660	733	802	839	1,089

[a]Weighted by students.

Table A.8

Distribution of Total Revenue per Pupil, by Race and Ethnicity:
Elementary School Districts in 1969–70
(in dollars)

Race/Ethnicity	Percentile[a]				
	5	25	50	75	95
Black	619	659	712	898	1,016
Hispanic	580	648	683	739	984
All	529	645	693	775	1,003

[a]Weighted by students.

Table A.9

Distribution of Total Revenue per Pupil, by Race and Ethnicity:
High School Districts in 1969–70
(in dollars)

Race/Ethnicity	Percentile[a]				
	5	25	50	75	95
Black	752	910	943	1,128	1,305
Hispanic	707	886	932	997	1,219
All	739	859	924	1,014	1,305

[a]Weighted by students.

Appendix B

Data Sources for Material in Chapter 3

School District Expenditures on Legislative Lobbyists

The data reported in Figure 3.8 are from *Lobbying Expenditures,* various years, California Secretary of State.

Federal Aid, Other Local Revenue, State Categorical Aid, State Noncategorical Aid, Property Taxes (Sum of All Districts)

The data in Figure 3.5 come from two sources. The first is the California State Controller's *Annual Report of Financial Transactions Concerning School Districts of California* for each fiscal year from 1969–70 to 1989–90. The second is the Governor's Budget for each fiscal year.

For fiscal years 1969–70 through 1986–87, we used the following definitions. Federal aid is the sum of federal total and combined state and federal total revenue from the Controller's report. Other local revenue is the sum of county total, sales and rentals, and other local revenue from the Controller's report. For 1969–70 through 1977–78, state noncategorical aid is the sum of basic aid, equalization aid, and supplementary aid for elementary schools and high schools from the Governor's Budget. For 1978–79 through 1991–92, state noncategorical aid is K–12 district revenue limit aid from the Governor's Budget. For 1969–70 through 1986–87, state categorical aid is the difference between total state aid, which is the sum of school fund apportionment and other state revenue from the Controller's report, and state noncategorical aid defined above. For 1987–88 through 1991–92, state categorical aid is other state revenue from the Controller's report. For 1969–70 through 1986–87, property taxes are the sum of district taxes, business inventory tax relief, homeowners tax relief, and other tax relief subventions. For 1987–88 through 1991–92, property taxes are the revenue limit sources from the Controller's report minus K–12 district revenue limit state aid from the Governor's Budget. From 1992–93 through 1996–97, all data are from the Controller's report. State categorical aid is the category called other state.

Revenue Limits

The revenue limits in Figure 3.3 and Tables B.1 through B.3 come from the following sources:

> 1974–75. "Estimated Revenue Limit per A.D.A." in Table 1, Selected 1974–75 Data, from *A Compilation of School District 1975–76 Revenue Limits Computed Pursuant to Senate Bill 90 and Assembly Bill 1267 by County Superintendents of Schools,* California State Department of Education, 1976.

1979–80. "79/80 Base Revenue Limit per ADA" in *A Compilation of School District and County 1979–80 Revenue Limits Computed by County Superintendents of Schools Pursuant to Assembly Bill 8, Chapter 282, Statutes of 1979*, California State Department of Education, 1980.

1984–85. "Base Revenue Limit per Unit of ADA" from *Selected Financial and Related Data for California Public Schools: Kindergarten Through Grade Twelve, 1984–85*, California State Department of Education, 1986.

1989–90. "Base Revenue Limit, Fiscal Year 89–90," from a data file provided by the California State Department of Education in 1999.

1994–95. "Base Revenue Limit, Fiscal Year 94–96," from a data file provided by the California State Department of Education in 1999.

Expenditures on Compensatory and Special Education

In Figure 3.5, the data on expenditures on compensatory and special education come from the Governor's Budget for 1976–77, 1981–82, 1986–87, 1991–92, 1996–97, and 1997–98. Expenditures on compensatory education are the sum of expenditures on the following programs: Bilingual Education (1974–75), Educationally Disadvantaged Youth (1974–75), Economic Impact Aid (1979–80, 1984–85, 1980–90, 1994–95, and 1996–97), Urban Impact Aid (1979–80 and 1984–85), Court Ordered Desegregation (1984–85, 1989–90, 1994–95, and 1996–97), and Voluntary Desegregation (1984–85, 1989–90, 1994–95, and 1996–97).

Total Revenue per Pupil (Individual Districts)

The data in Figure 3.6 and Table B.4 through B.6 for 1964–65 through 1984–85 come from the California State Controller's *Annual Report of Financial Transactions Concerning School Districts of California.* For 1989–90 and 1994–95, the data come from the J201 database of the California State Department of Education.

Supplementary Figures and Tables for Chapter 3

The growth rate in revenue limits, depicted in Figure 3.3 for unified districts, is shown in Figure B.1 for elementary school districts and in Figure B.2 for high school districts.

The convergence in revenue limits, depicted in Figure 3.4 for unified districts, is shown for all districts in Tables B.1, B.2, and B.3.

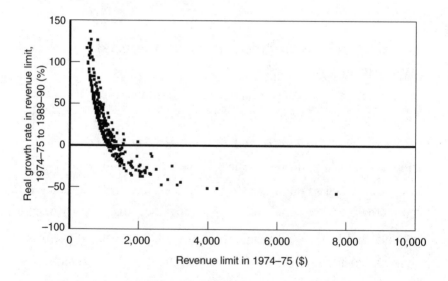

Figure B.1—Growth Rate in Revenue Limits: Elementary School Districts

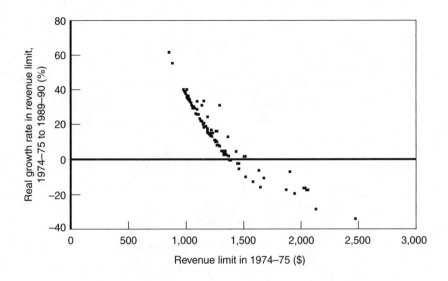

Figure B.2—Growth Rate in Revenue Limits: High School Districts

Table B.1

Revenue Limit per Pupil: Unified Districts

Year	Percentile[a]				75/25	95/5
	5	25	75	95		
1974–75	$844	$880	$997	$1,278	1.13	1.51
1979–80	1,485	1,542	1,646	1,781	1.07	1.20
1984–85	2,176	2,176	2,195	2,308	1.01	1.06
1989–90	2,911	2,919	2,947	3,116	1.01	1.07
1994–95	3,461	3,469	3,500	3,727	1.01	1.08

[a]Weighted by district enrollment.

The convergence of total revenue per pupil, depicted in Figure 3.6 for unified districts, is shown in Tables B.4, B.5, and B.6 for all districts.

Table B.2

Revenue Limit per Pupil: Elementary School Districts

Year	Percentile[a]				75/25	95/5
	5	25	75	95		
1974–75	$719	$799	$909	$1,199	1.14	1.67
1979–80	1,341	1,390	1,504	1,645	1.08	1.23
1984–85	2,023	2,023	2,046	2,339	1.01	1.16
1989–90	2,716	2,722	2,750	3,202	1.01	1.18
1994–95	3,236	3,242	3,271	3,722	1.01	1.15

[a]Weighted by district enrollment.

Table B.3

Revenue Limit per Pupil: High School Districts

Year	Percentile[a]				75/25	95/5
	5	25	75	95		
1974–75	$892	$1,034	$1,248	$1,643	1.21	1.84
1979–80	1,485	1,542	1,646	1,782	1.07	1.20
1984–85	2,499	2,511	2,547	2,833	1.01	1.13
1989–90	3,372	3,384	3,406	3,662	1.01	1.09
1994–95	4,007	4,027	4,046	4,307	1.01	1.07

[a]Weighted by district enrollment.

Table B.4

Distribution of Total Revenue per Pupil: Unified Districts

Year	Percentile[a]				75/25	95/5
	5	25	75	95		
1964–65	$448	$ 490	$ 541	$ 628	1.10	1.40
1969–70	669	733	839	1,089	1.14	1.63
1974–75	1,078	1,152	1,300	1,567	1.13	1.45
1979–80	1,837	1,967	2,355	2,580	1.20	1.40
1984–85	2,742	2,871	3,349	3,359	1.17	1.23
1989–90	3,913	4,071	4,894	5,003	1.20	1.28
1994–95	3,998	4,213	5,070	5,423	1.20	1.36
1997–98	5,071	5,298	6,235	6,660	1.18	1.31

[a]Weighted by district enrollment.

Table B.5

Distribution of Total Revenue per Pupil: Elementary School Districts

Year	Percentile[a]				75/25	95/5
	5	25	75	95		
1964–65	$ 371	$ 404	$ 488	$ 599	1.21	1.61
1969–70	582	645	775	1,003	1.20	1.72
1974–75	991	1,053	1,304	1,584	1.24	1.60
1979–80	1,680	1,831	2,127	2,547	1.16	1.52
1984–85	2,513	2,687	2,943	3,551	1.10	1.41
1989–90	3,494	3,695	4,016	4,530	1.09	1.30
1994–95	3,694	3,912	4,239	4,626	1.08	1.25
1997–98	4,831	5,151	5,631	6,124	1.09	1.27

[a]Weighted by district enrollment.

Table B.6

Distribution of Total Revenue per Pupil: High School Districts

Year	Percentile[a]				75/25	95/5
	5	25	75	95		
1964–65	$ 531	$ 567	$ 715	$ 859	1.26	1.62
1969–70	739	859	1,014	1,305	1.18	1.77
1974–75	1,021	1,139	1,460	1,748	1.28	1.71
1979–80	1,837	2,010	2,332	2,698	1.16	1.46
1984–85	3,007	3,152	3,483	4,175	1.11	1.39
1989–90	4,566	4,723	5,358	6,125	1.13	1.34
1994–95	4,584	4,855	5,278	6,388	1.09	1.39
1997–98	5,464	5,777	6,228	7,520	1.08	1.38

[a]Weighted by district enrollment.

Appendix C
Data Sources for Material in Chapter 4

School District Revenues

For 1989–90, the source for school district revenues was the J201 data tape provided by the California Department of Education. The tape gives revenues from all categories for each school district in 1989–90. The amounts in each district were summed to yield the totals reported in Tables 4.1 and 4.3. The only exception is the Desegregation Program. In the J201 data tape, revenues from this program are reported with other revenues in the category "Mandated Costs Reimbursements." The total for the Desegregation Program listed in Table 4.1 was taken from the Governor's Budget: 1990–91. The data on district revenue in Tables 4.4, 4.5, 4.6, and 4.7 also come from the J201 tape.

Revenue Limits for 1974–75

The 1974–75 revenue limits reported in Tables 4.6 and 4.7 are from *A Compilation of School District 1975–76 Revenue Limits Computed Pursuant to Senate Bill 90 and Assembly Bill 1267 by County Superintendents of Schools*, California State Department of Education, 1976.

State Expenditures on Court Ordered Desegregation

Data in Table 4.2 are from *Desegregation Funding Options: A Report to the Legislature As Requested in the Supplemental Report of the 1990 Budget Act, Item 6110-114-001 and Item 6110-115-001*, prepared by the California State Department of Education, March 22, 1991.

Family Income

The data on family income in Figure 4.1 are from the file of the "School District Data Book," produced by the National Center for Education Statistics, U.S. Department of Education.

Race and Ethnicity

The data on student race and ethnicity in Figure 4.2 are from the Website of the California Department of Education.

Supplementary Tables for Chapter 4

Revenue sources by quartile, given in Table 4.4 for unified districts and in Table 4.5 for elementary school districts, are shown in Table C.1 for high school districts.

The distribution of revenue per pupil by family income, depicted in Figure 4.1, is shown in more detail in Tables C.2, C.3, C.4, and C.5.

Table C.1

Revenue Sources of Total Revenue per Pupil, by Quartile:
High School Districts in 1989–90
(in dollars)

Quartile	Revenue Limit Funds per Pupil	State Categorical Aid per Pupil	Federal Aid per Pupil	Other Local Revenue per Pupil	Total Revenue per Pupil
First quartile 0–4,722	3,628	721	141	156	4,646
Second quartile 4,723–4,998	3,724	768	165	214	4,871
Third quartile 4,999–5,358	3,728	840	188	319	5,075
Fourth quartile 5,359 and above	4,162	983	212	497	5,854

Table C.2

Distribution of Total Revenue per Pupil, by Family Income Group:
Unified Districts in 1989–90
(in dollars)

| Income | Percentile[a] | | | | |
	5	25	50	75	95
0–9,999	3,946	4,144	4,486	5,003	5,003
10,000–19,999	3,945	4,134	4,352	5,003	5,003
20,000–27,499	3,938	4,114	4,298	5,003	5,003
27,500–34,999	3,935	4,091	4,272	4,923	5,003
35,000–44,999	3,927	4,074	4,228	4,894	5,003
45,000–59,999	3,913	4,059	4,212	4,894	5,003
60,000–99,999	3,913	4,046	4,200	4,894	5,003
100,000 and above	3,935	4,065	4,309	5,003	5,003

[a]Weighted by families.

Table C.3

Distribution of Total Revenue per Pupil, by Family Income Group: Elementary School Districts in 1989–90
(in dollars)

Income	Percentile[a]				
	5	25	50	75	95
0–9,999	3,548	3,702	3,875	4,001	4,488
10,000–19,999	3,534	3,692	3,874	4,016	4,488
20,000–27,499	3,524	3,685	3,874	4,016	4,530
27,500–34,999	3,496	3,680	3,872	4,001	4,530
35,000–44,999	3,495	3,676	3,861	4,016	4,530
45,000–59,999	3,490	3,670	3,845	4,020	4,535
60,000–99,999	3,488	3,684	3,872	4,065	4,603
100,000 and above	3,494	3,739	3,878	4,251	4,941

[a]Weighted by families.

Table C.4

Distribution of Total Revenue per Pupil, by Family Income Group: High School Districts in 1989–90
(in dollars)

Income	Percentile[a]				
	5	25	50	75	95
0–9,999	4,556	4,724	4,999	5,407	6,038
10,000–19,999	4,566	4,724	5,007	5,407	6,038
20,000–27,499	4,513	4,724	4,999	5,407	6,125
27,500–34,999	4,513	4,724	4,999	5,407	6,125
35,000–44,999	4,513	4,723	4,999	5,407	6,125
45,000–59,999	4,513	4,723	4,998	5,411	6,125
60,000–99,999	4,513	4,724	4,999	5,411	6,125
100,000 and above	4,566	4,851	5,054	5,563	6,168

[a]Weighted by families.

Table C.5

Distribution of Total Revenue per Pupil, by Family Income Group:
Unified Districts and Selected Counties[a] in 1989–90
(in dollars)

Income	Percentile[b]				
	5	25	50	75	95
0–9,999	3,942	4,143	4,360	5,003	5,003
10,000–19,999	3,942	4,143	4,343	5,003	5,003
20,000–27,499	3,941	4,121	4,303	4,923	5,003
27,500–34,999	3,886	4,103	4,272	4,894	5,003
35,000–44,999	3,927	4,074	4,230	4,894	5,003
45,000–59,999	3,916	4,070	4,226	4,868	5,003
60,000–99,999	3,913	4,064	4,217	4,894	5,003
100,000 and above	3,940	4,071	4,343	5,003	5,003

[a]Unified districts plus 12 counties without district-level census data.
[b]Weighted by families.

The distribution of revenue per pupil by race and ethnicity, depicted in Figure 4.2, is shown in more detail in Tables C.6, C.7, and C.8.

Table C.6

Distribution of Total Revenue per Pupil, by Race and Ethnicity:
Unified Districts in 1989–90
(in dollars)

Race/Ethnicity	Percentile[a]				
	5	25	50	75	95
Black students	3,941	4,185	4,486	5,003	5,003
Hispanic students	3,938	4,134	4,316	5,003	5,003
All students	3,913	4,071	4,228	4,894	5,003

[a]Weighted by families.

Table C.7

Distribution of Total Revenue per Pupil, by Race and Ethnicity: Elementary School Districts in 1989–90
(in dollars)

Race/Ethnicity	Percentile[a]				
	5	25	50	75	95
Black students	3,553	3,716	3,887	4,037	4,808
Hispanic students	3,596	3,729	3,887	4,037	4,366
All students	3,494	3,693	3,856	4,016	4,530

[a]Weighted by students.

Table C.8

Distribution of Total Revenue per Pupil, by Race and Ethnicity: High School Districts in 1989–90
(in dollars)

Race/Ethnicity	Percentile[a]				
	5	25	50	75	95
Black students	4,513	4,723	4,999	5,354	6,038
Hispanic students	4,652	4,715	4,999	5,358	5,812
All students	4,556	4,723	4,998	5,358	6,125

[a]Weighted by students.

Appendix D

Data Sources for Material in Chapter 5

Public School Spending, Public School Pupils, and State Population

In Figures 5.1, 5.3, and 5.5, public school spending consists of current expenditures on public elementary and secondary schools. For 1969–70 through 1989–90, this measure is from *Historical Trends: State Education Facts 1969 to 1989,* National Center for Education Statistics. For 1990–91 through 1997–98, it is from the *Digest of Education Statistics: 1998,* National Center for Education Statistics.

In Figures 5.1 and 5.2, the number of pupils is the enrollment in public elementary and secondary schools. For 1969 through 1989, this measure is from *Historical Trends: State Education Facts 1969 to 1989.* For 1990 through 1997, it is from the *Digest of Education Statistics: 1998.*

In Figures 5.2, 5.3, 5.4, and 5.6, state population is from the "State Annual Summary Tables," Bureau of Economic Analysis Website, U.S. Department of Commerce.

In Table 5.1, spending per pupil consists of total general fund expenditures divided by average daily attendance. Both measures are from the California State Controller's *Annual Report of Financial Transactions Concerning School Districts of California: Fiscal Year 1969–70.* This measure of spending per pupil is used in the regressions reported below.

Personal Income

In Figures 5.4 and 5.5, personal income is from the "State Annual Summary Tables," Bureau of Economic Analysis Website, U.S. Department of Commerce.

Direct, Current Expenditures by State and Local Governments

In Figure 5.6, direct, current expenditures are direct, general, current expenditures from *Government Finances,* U.S. Bureau of the Census, annual editions from 1969–70 through 1995–96.

Median Family Income

In the demand regressions reported below, median family income is calculated from the income distribution for each district reported in "1970 Census Fourth Count: School District Data Tapes." The Census reported data on 740 of the 1,080 districts in 1969–70. Total enrollment of the 340 districts not included in the Census data was

78,407, which is 1.7 percent of the total number of public school students in California. All but five of the districts not included in the Census had enrollment fewer than 500 students. The five districts with enrollments of more than 500 students (the largest had 17,000) were all involved in consolidations between 1969 and 1971.

Assessed Value per Pupil

In Table 5.1 and in the regressions reported below, assessed value is total assessed value divided by average daily attendance. Both measures are from the California State Controller's *Annual Report of Financial Transactions Concerning School Districts of California: Fiscal Year 1969–70.*

Statistical Results

Model

Let y be a family's income, and let h be the assessed value of the family's house. Assume that $h = \alpha y^{\theta}$. The family's tax price for spending per pupil is $p = h / v$, where v is assessed value per pupil. Assume that the family's demand function is $s = \beta p^{\varepsilon} y^{n}$. Substituting the function for assessed value into the demand function yields $s = \beta \alpha^{\varepsilon} v^{-\varepsilon} y^{n + \varepsilon \theta}$. Following Borcherding and Deacon (1972) and Bergstrom and Goodman (1973), assume that the median income voter is decisive. This leads to the following regression: The dependent variable is the log of spending per pupil and the independent variables are the log of assessed value per pupil and the log of median family income. The coefficient on assessed value per pupil is the elasticity of spending per pupil with respect to the tax price.

Regression Results

Table D.1

Elementary School, High School, and Unified Districts

Variable	Elementary School Districts		High School Districts		Unified Districts	
	Coef.	S. E.	Coef.	S. E.	Coef.	S. E.
Log of assessed value per pupil	0.171	0.013	0.265	0.025	0.267	0.015
Log of median family income	0.137	0.029	0.002	0.043	0.035	0.033
Constant	3.650	0.282	4.121	0.481	3.888	0.333
Observations	401		110		228	
Adj. R-squared	0.346		0.508		0.569	

Appendix E

Data Sources for Material in Chapter 6

Average Teachers' Salaries, Current Expenditures, and Pupils per Teacher

The data in Figures 6.1, 6.2, and 6.3 are from *Historical Trends: State Education Facts 1969 to 1989*, *Digest of Education Statistics: 1994*, *Digest of Education Statistics: 1996*, and *Digest of Education Statistics: 1998*. All are published by the National Center of Education Statistics.

Income and Characteristics of Teachers and Nonteachers

The data used in the regressions described in Tables 6.1, 6.2, and 6.3 are from the "1970 Census of Population Public Use Microdata 15 Percent Sample," the "1980 Census of Population and Housing Public Use Microdata 5 Percent Sample," and the "1990 Census of Population and Housing Public Use Microdata 5 Percent Sample." From those samples, we excluded individuals who did not have a bachelor's degree, who worked less than 27 weeks in the previous year, whose usual hours of work per week were less than 35, and those who had self-employment income. The dependent variable in our regressions is a person's salary. For 1970, that variable is "wages, salary, commissions, bonuses, or tips from all jobs." For 1980 and 1990, the variable is "wage or salary income."

The regressors in those regressions are defined as follows:

Age	Age of person in years.
Age squared	Square of age.
Full year	Person worked 48 weeks or more in previous year.
Secondary	Unity if person is a secondary school teacher, zero otherwise.
Bachelor's plus	Unity if person has education beyond a bachelor's, zero otherwise.
In school	Unity if person is attending school, zero otherwise.
Nonwhite	Unity if person is not white or is Hispanic, zero otherwise.
Children	For females, the number of children ever born.

Appendix F

Data Sources for Material in Chapter 7

Demographic Data for California and the United States

Demographic data on the population of California and the United States in 1970, 1980, and 1990 are from the U.S. Bureau of the Census, *Statistical Abstract of the United States,* selected years.

National Assessment of Educational Progress

The data for Table 7.1 are from the "1992 Trial State Assessment in Reading."

The definitions of the variables used in the regression analysis are: dummies for white, black, Hispanic, or Asian; whether the respondent's father completed high school only or college; whether the respondent's mother completed high school only or college; whether the primary language spoken in the respondent's home is English; and whether the respondent was born in the United States.

National Education Longitudinal Study of 1988, High School and Beyond, and the National Longitudinal Study of the High School Class of 1972

The NELS, HSB, and NLS surveys provide a battery of test results for participants. The scores were added together to form a single test score for each student, which was then standardized to a mean of 50 and a standard deviation of 10. The data included dummies for white, black, Hispanic or Latino, and Asian; whether the respondent's father completed high school only or college; whether the respondent's mother completed high school only or college; and whether English was the language spoken at the student's home.

The income variables were constructed from a question on family income. Each respondent who answered placed his or her family into an income category. These categories were reclassified to separate all respondents into quartiles, so that income1 is a dummy representing students who placed their family in the lowest income quartile, income2 represents approximately the second quartile, etc. Because the original categories do not precisely map into quartiles, the variables differ slightly from NELS to HSB to NLS.

Scholastic Aptitude Test

The average SAT scores, incomes, and racial/ethnic breakdowns of the test-takers for each state are from *Profile of SAT and Achievement Test Takers,* various years and states, published by the Educational Testing

Service. Data for 1986 were not available. The number of test-takers was combined with data from the Department of Education on the number of high school graduates by state to generate a participation rate for each state for each year.

Calculation of Adjusted Test Scores

To compare the performance of California's median student with the performance of students in other states, the scores were first adjusted for the demographics of the test-takers using the following procedure.

For the NAEP, NELS, HSB, and NLS, we first estimated a regression of test scores on the set of demographic controls described above:

$$Y = X\hat{\beta} + \hat{u}$$

The adjusted test scores for each student were calculated by replacing the actual demographic data with the average characteristics of all respondents:

$$Y_{ADJ} = \overline{X}\hat{\beta} + \hat{u}$$

These adjusted scores were calculated for all students in the United States, including those in California. We then found the median student in California and determined what his or her percentile ranking would have been in the rest of the country. Because the adjusted scores for all students use the same demographic characteristics, in effect we are simply comparing the estimated residuals. A positive residual indicates that a student scored higher than we would expect given his or her characteristics; if California's students had generally positive residuals it would indicate that they were scoring better than similar students in the rest of the country.

For the SAT, the dependent variable was the average SAT score for each state rather than test score for individual students. Following Dynarski and Gleason (1993) and Graham and Husted (1993), the regressions included controls for race and ethnicity, mean income, and the participation rate in cubic form. Dynarski and Gleason found that adjusting for participation rates provided scores that were highly correlated with state rankings based on the 1990 NAEP. The pre- and post-1986 datasets contained different racial/ethnic definitions, and the relevant racial categories were interacted with a dummy indicating pre- or post-1986.

Supplementary Tables for Chapter 7

The estimates of the adjusted score for California were calculated using the regression coefficients from Table F.6. The estimates of the adjusted scores are somewhat sensitive to the specification of the model. Including year dummies does not materially change the results, but changing the manner in which the race and ethnicity variables are included can lead to different estimates. Nevertheless, in all cases there is a decline in California's performance between the early 1980s and the early 1990s, which mirrors the decline in the unadjusted test scores (see Table F.1).

Test scores were adjusted for demographic differences using a regression of test scores of socioeconomic characteristics. Table F.2 gives the regression results for the 1992 NAEP.

Table F.1

SAT Scores

Year	United States Except California	California	California Adjusted
1980	891	896	897
1981	891	901	899
1982	894	899	898
1983	893	895	893
1984	899	897	897
1985	907	904	905
1986	—	—	—
1987	905	906	902
1988	904	908	901
1989	903	906	901
1990	899	903	897
1991	895	897	889
1992	897	900	893
1993	902	899	894
1994	902	895	893
1995	910	902	902

Table F.2

1992 NAEP Regression Results

Variable	Coef.	S. E.
White	17.45	3.31
Black	−11.97	3.54
Hispanic	−0.018	3.57
Asian	14.60	4.35
DadHS	2.32	1.32
DadColl	9.71	1.54
MomHS	6.49	1.41
MomColl	9.04	1.42
Enghome	3.27	1.13
BornUS	15.96	1.82
Constant	180.67	3.14
No. of obs.		5,045

NOTE: The omitted race/ethnicity category is other or missing.

The sampling methodology used in NAEP and the use of plausible values require unusual estimation procedures for both coefficients and standard errors. The procedures are fully outlined in the *1992 Trial State Assessment Program in Reading Secondary-Use Data Files User Guide*.

The coefficient estimates are calculated as the average of five estimates generated using each of the five plausible values of reading proficiency provided for each student.

The standard errors are estimated with a jackknife technique. Each regression is first estimated with each of the five plausible values. This procedure is then repeated 215 times using a set of replicate weights provided with the data to approximate a new draw of data from the entire sample. The standard errors are then calculated from the standard deviations of the estimates. The estimated standard errors are not consistent.

The 1988 NELS test scores were adjusted for demographic differences using the regression results in Table F.3.

The 1980 HSB test scores were adjusted for demographic differences using the regression results in Table F.4.

The 1972 NLS test scores were adjusted for demographic differences using the regression results in Table F.5.

The SAT scores were adjusted for differences in demographics and participation rates using the regression results in Table F.6. The regressions were weighted using the number of test-takers in each state. The pre- and post-1986 datasets contained different racial/ethnic definitions, and the relevant variables (% other and % Hispanic were interacted with a post-1987 dummy). The omitted category was %

Table F.3

1988 NELS Regression Results

Variable	Coef.	Robust S. E.
White	5.70	0.42
Black	–0.31	0.44
Hispanic	1.64	0.45
Asian	5.49	0.52
Income1	–0.98	0.25
Income2	1.33	0.24
Income3	2.68	0.26
Income4	3.69	0.27
DadHS	1.46	0.17
DadColl	3.57	0.20
MomHS	1.97	0.17
MomColl	3.97	0.25
Enghome	–0.38	0.21
Constant	40.7	0.45
No. of obs.		23,431

NOTE: The omitted race/ethnicity and income categories are race equal to other or missing and income missing.

white. The estimated coefficients and residuals were then used to generate adjusted SAT scores for each state for each year. Those adjusted scores were used to generate Table 7.6 and Figure 7.2. Including year dummies does not materially change the results.

The test scores of low-income students were adjusted for demographic differences using the regression results reported in Table F.7. The regressions included only students in the lowest income quartile. These coefficients were used to calculate the adjusted scores following the procedure described above.

Table F.4

1980 HSB Regression Results

Variable	Coef.	Robust S. E.
White	3.52	0.26
Black	−2.80	0.29
Hispanic	−3.77	0.23
Asian	5.40	0.73
Income1	−0.56	0.20
Income2	1.67	0.18
Income3	1.93	0.22
Income4	2.75	0.21
DadHS	1.38	0.14
DadColl	5.39	0.22
MomHS	2.12	0.14
MomColl	4.81	0.25
Enghome	−1.35	0.20
Constant	44.55	0.29
No. of obs.		26,986

NOTE: The omitted race/ethnicity and income categories are race equal to other or missing and income missing.

The regression reported in Table F.8 was also estimated with a dummy variable for California. The regressions included only students in the lowest income quartile. In NLS and HSB, the estimated coefficient on the California dummy is insignificant. In the NELS sample, the estimated coefficient is negative and significant.

Table F.5

1972 NLS Regression Results

Variable	Coef.	Robust S. E.
White	5.97	0.43
Black	–3.19	0.47
Hispanic	–0.22	0.55
Asian	7.19	0.88
Income1	0.68	0.24
Income2	2.42	0.23
Income3	2.75	0.27
Income4	3.37	0.25
DadHS	1.98	0.19
DadColl	5.29	0.27
MomHS	2.71	0.20
MomColl	4.52	0.33
Enghome	1.52	0.28
Constant	38.0	0.50
No. of obs.		15,840

NOTE: The omitted race/ethnicity and income categories are race equal to other or missing and income missing.

Table F.6

SAT Regression Results

Variable	Coef.	Robust S. E.
% other pre-1987	7.24	2.49
% other post-1987	1.76	1.31
(% other pre-1987)^2	−0.53	0.27
(% other post-1987)^2	−0.15	0.08
% black	−2.61	0.42
% black^2	−0.01	0.02
% Asian	2.71	0.35
(% Asian)^2	−0.05	0.01
% Hispanic pre-1987	−7.16	1.88
% Hispanic post-1987	−6.35	1.00
(% Hispanic pre-1987)^2	0.24	0.16
(% Hispanic post-1987)^2	0.28	0.06
Mean income	1.53	0.18
Participation rate	−678	53
(Participation rate)^2	939	132
(Participation rate)^3	−453	94
Constant	1004	10
No. of obs.		594

Table F.7

NLS, HSB, and NELS Low-Income Regression Results

Variable	NLS Coef.	NLS Robust S. E.	HSB Coef.	HSB Robust S. E.	NELS Coef.	NELS Robust S. E.
White	5.78	0.78	2.50	0.57	5.23	0.67
Black	–3.20	0.79	–2.36	0.60	–0.39	0.67
Hispanic	0.63	0.91	–3.20	0.43	1.55	0.72
Asian	5.61	2.12	4.30	1.66	3.01	0.99
DadHS	1.51	0.37	0.47	0.34	1.53	0.31
DadColl	3.72	0.87	1.14	0.84	2.34	0.65
MomHS	3.21	0.37	2.38	0.30	2.15	0.30
MomColl	4.11	1.07	5315	0.90	2.34	0.65
Enghome	2.47	0.54	–1.16	0.48	–0.61	0.45
Constant	38.0	0.85	44.6	0.57	40.4	0.69
No. of obs.		3,879		4,524		4,185

NOTE: The omitted race/ethnicity and income categories are race equal to other or missing and income missing.

Table F.8

NLS, HSB, and NELS Low-Income Regression Results, with California Dummy Variable

Variable	NLS Coef.	NLS Robust S. E.	HSB Coef.	HSB Robust S. E.	NELS Coef.	NELS Robust S. E.
White	5.80	0.66	2.54	0.51	5.21	0.64
Black	–3.18	0.70	–2.32	0.55	–0.43	0.66
Hispanic	0.58	0.85	–3.20	0.44	1.62	0.71
Asian	5.53	1.64	4.22	1.32	3.33	0.94
DadHS	1.49	0.31	0.48	0.29	1.54	0.27
DadColl	3.68	0.85	1.13	0.64	3.55	0.65
MomHS	3.21	0.31	2.37	0.26	2.13	0.27
MomColl	4.10	0.89	5.14	0.66	2.35	0.57
Enghome	2.46	0.48	–1.14	0.40	–0.65	0.40
Constant	38.0	0.75	44.5	0.53	40.5	0.68
California dummy	0.27	0.53	0.38	0.48	–0.98	0.44
No. of obs.		3,879		4,524		4,185

NOTE: The omitted race/ethnicity and income categories are race equal to other or missing and income missing.

Appendix G

Data Sources for Material in Chapter 8

Public and Private School Enrollment Rates

For the United States, total enrollment in public and private elementary and secondary schools is from Table 3 of the *Digest of Education Statistics 1997*, National Center for Education Statistics. For California, enrollment in public elementary and secondary schools from 1970 to 1988 is from Table 1 of *Historical Trends: State Education Facts 1969 to 1989*, National Center for Education Statistics. The data for 1989 to 1995 are from Table 40 of the *Digest of Education Statistics 1997*, National Center for Education Statistics. Private school enrollment for California is from the Office of District and School Program Coordination, California Department of Education.

Private School Enrollment by Family Income

The data for 1970 are from the 1970 Census of Population and Housing, Public Use Microdata Samples, 15 Percent State Sample. The data for 1980 and 1990 are from the Census of Population and Housing, Public Use Microdata 5 Percent Samples.

Appendix H

Data Sources for Material in Chapter 9

1994–95 School and School District Enrollments

The data on 1994–95 school and district enrollments are from "Education Demographics," California Department of Education Website.

1974–75 Revenue Limits

The 1974–75 revenue limit data in Tables 9.3, 9.4, and H.1 are from *A Compilation of School District 1975–76 Revenue Limits Computed Pursuant to Senate Bill 90 and Assembly Bill 1267 by County Superintendents of Schools*, California State Department of Education, 1976.

School-Level Average Family Income

The family income data listed in Figure 9.2 and Tables 9.5 and H.2 are from the "1990 Census Summary Tape File 3 (STF3)," U.S. Bureau of the Census, Department of Commerce.

To link schools to Census tracts, we obtained the physical address of each school in California from the California Department of Education and geocoded the addresses to identify the Census tract in which each school was located. Using this procedure, we were able to uniquely match 92 percent (6,553/7,124) of the schools operating in California in 1994–95 to a Census tract. Of the 571 schools that we were unable to match to a Census tract, 408 were elementary or middle schools and 163 were junior or senior high schools.

District-Level Average Family Income

The data listed in Figure 9.3 and Table 9.6 are from "School District Data Book [CD-ROM]," Office of Educational Research and Improvement, National Center for Educational Statistics, U.S. Department of Education, Washington, D.C., 1994.

The "Data Book" included family income data on 779 of the 1,001 school districts operating in California in 1994–95. Of the 222 school districts for which there were no family income data, 202 were located in one of the 12 counties that were excluded from the "Data Book." The remaining 20 represent districts that were either newly formed or underwent consolidation between 1989–90 and 1994–95.

Supplementary Tables for Chapter 9

The relationship between contributions and revenue limits, shown in Figure 9.3 for elementary school districts and in Figure 9.4 for unified districts, is given in Table H.1 for high school districts.

The relationship between family income and contributions, shown for elementary and middle schools, in Table 9.5, is given for junior and senior high schools in Table H.2.

Table H.1

Contributions per Pupil, by Quartiles of 1974–75 Revenue Limits: High School Districts

	School-Level Contributions[a]		District-Level Contributions[a]	
Quartile	% with Revenue of $25,000 or More	Average Revenue per Pupil ($)	% with Revenue of $25,000 or More	Average Revenue per Pupil ($)
First quartile 0–1,069[b]	27	72	12	6
Second quartile 1,070–1,199	18	139	4	8
Third quartile 1,200–1,299	24	112	8	12
Fourth quartile 1,300 and above[c]	20	64	20	36

[a]1994 tax year.

[b]Twenty-five percent of the high school districts operating in California in 1994–95 had a 1974–75 revenue limit less than or equal to this number.

[c]Twenty-five percent of the high school districts operating in California in 1994–95 had a 1974–75 revenue limit greater than or equal to this number.

Table H.2

Family Income and Contributions[a] per Pupil: Junior and Senior High Schools

1990 Average Family Income ($)	% with Revenue of $25,000 or More	Average Revenue per Pupil ($)	% with Revenue of $25,000 or More	Average Revenue per Pupil ($)
0–29,999	11	107	2.4	351
30,000–49,999	14	106	3.7	317
50,000–69,999	29	141	9.0	367
70,000–99,999	44	163	19.1	321
100,000 and above	62	117	22.0	245

[a]1994 tax year.

Appendix I

Data Sources for Material in Chapter 10

Number of School Districts and School District Enrollments

Data on school district enrollments and the number of school districts in Los Angeles and Orange County, California, are from the California State Controller's *Annual Report of Financial Transactions Concerning School Districts of California*, for fiscal year 1989–90.

Number of Families and Average Family Income

These data were from the "School District Data Book [CD-ROM]," Office of Educational Research and Improvement, National Center for Educational Statistics, U.S. Department of Education, Washington, D.C., 1994.

Time to Work, Percentage of Population Age 65 and Older, and Percentage of Population Below Poverty Level

The data in Table 10.1 are from the "1990 Census Summary Tape File 3 (STF3)," U.S. Bureau of the Census, Department of Commerce.

Beach

The data on number of miles to the nearest beach reported in Table 10.1 were generated by calculating the linear distance from the centroid of each Census tract to the nearest beach. Each single-family home in a specific Census tract was then assigned the same value for number of miles to the nearest beach.

Annual Average of Total Suspended Particulates

These data were generated in the following manner: First, the air pollution data, obtained from monitoring station or airport readings, are aggregated into an annual average. Second, these summary data are entered into the SURFER computer program to generate isopleth contours. Third, the isopleths are used to create pollution levels at grid points that cover the entire study area. Fourth, each Census tract is assigned the pollution level of the grid point that is closest to its centroid. Finally, each single-family home in a specific Census tract is assigned the same pollution value.

Supplementary Tables for Chapter 10

The premiums for all districts in our sample are given in Table I.1.

Table I.1

School District Premiums[a]

	Premium (%)
Los Angeles County	
ABC Unified	5.4
Arcadia Unified	44.4
Azusa Unified	17.1
Baldwin Park Unified	10.3
Bassett Unified	5.8
Bellflower Unified	−5.4
Beverly Hills Unified	40.5
Bonita Unified	34.7
Burbank Unified	2.1
Charter Oak Unified	19.8
Claremont Unified	21.4
Compton Unified	−21.7
Covina-Valley Unified	14.0
Culver City Unified	7.1
Downey Unified	4.5
Duarte Unified	17.5
East Whittier City Elementary	−6.5
El Monte City Elementary	21.9
El Rancho Unified	0.1
El Segundo Unified	−23.5
Garvey Elementary	21.4
Glendale Unified	29.8
Glendora Unified	32.3
Hawthorne Elementary	−17.2
Hermosa Beach City Elementary	27.2
Inglewood Unified	−23.1
La Canada Unified	40.4
Lawndale Elementary	−15.2
Lennox Elementary	−19.4
Little Lake City Elementary	−4.0
Long Beach Unified	−9.4
Los Nietos Elementary	−8.6
Lynwood Unified	0.5
Monrovia Unified	23.0
Montebello Unified	15.9
Mountain View Elementary	24.8
Newhall Elementary	3.9
Norwalk–La Mirada Unified	−10.5

Table I.1 (continued)

	Premium (%)
Palos Verdes Peninsula Unified	31.6
Paramount Unified	−7.2
Pasadena Unified	21.5
Pomona Unified	10.5
Rosemead Elementary	24.6
Rowland Unified	21.8
San Marino Unified	45.5
Santa Monica–Malibu Unified	25.1
Saugus Union Elementary	13.1
South Pasadena Unified	33.3
South Whittier Elementary	−0.5
Sulphur Springs Union Elementary	10.2
Temple City Unified	19.4
Torrance Unified	−1.8
Valle Lindo Elementary	20.1
Walnut Valley Unified	34.9
West Covina Unified	17.6
Whittier City Elementary	0.0
Wiseburn Elementary	−20.6
Orange County	
Anaheim Elementary	−4.4
Brea-Olinda Unified	10.0
Buena Park Elementary	6.5
Centralia Elementary	5.1
Cypress Elementary	7.7
Fountain Valley Elementary	−6.7
Fullerton Elementary	8.2
Garden Grove Unified	−2.6
Huntington Beach City Elementary	9.0
Irvine Unified	7.0
La Habra City Elementary	3.1
Laguna Beach Unified	43.4
Newport-Mesa Unified	11.9
Ocean View Elementary	11.0
Orange Unified	7.7
Santa Ana Unified	5.0
Savanna Elementary	2.1
Tustin Unified	−4.2
Westminster Elementary	1.8

[a]Percentage premium measured relative to Los Angeles Unified School District.

The premiums reported in Table I.1 are parameter estimates from a regression of the logarithm of a house's sale price on school district dummy variables and other characteristics. The parameter estimates for other characteristics are given in Table I.2.

Table I.2

Estimated Hedonic Equations: Dependent Variable = Ln(House Sale Price)

	Coefficient[a]
Structural characteristics	
No. of bathrooms	0.06
Presence of central air conditioning (yes=1, no=0)	0.06
No. of fireplaces	0.07
Age of home	−0.00009
Lot area in square feet	0.0000014
Interior living space in square feet	0.00035
Presence of pool (yes=1, no=0)	0.07
Presence of a view (yes=1, no=0)	0.09
Neighborhood characteristics	
% in Census tract above 65 years old	0.005
Miles to nearest beach	−0.015
% in Census tract below poverty level	−0.012
Per capita FBI crime index	−0.001
Time to work in minutes	−0.015
Annual average of total suspended particulates (parts per million)	−0.005
Intercept	12.79
R-squared	0.55
No. of obs.	41,852

[a]All coefficients are significantly different from 0 at the 5 percent level.

Bibliography

Alexander, Arthur J., and Gail V. Bass, *Schools, Taxes, and Voter Behavior: An Analysis of School District Property Tax Elections*, RAND, Santa Monica, California, R-1465-FF, April 1974.

Barro, Stephen M., *Alternatives in California School Finance*, RAND, Santa Monica, California, R-663-RC/CC, May 1971.

Bergstrom, Theodore C., and Robert P. Goodman, "Private Demands for Public Goods," *American Economic Review*, Vol. 63, 1973, pp. 280–296.

Bergstrom, Theodore C., Daniel L. Rubinfeld, and Perry Shapiro, "Micro-Based Estimates of Demand Functions for Local School Expenditures," *Econometrica*, Vol. 50, September 1982, pp. 1183–1205.

Berman, Weiler Associates, *Improving School Improvement: An Independent Evaluation of the California School Improvement Program*, Berkeley, California, April 1983.

Beron, Kurt J., James C. Murdoch, and Mark A. Thayer, *Improving Visibility Benefit Estimates from Hedonic Models*, Report of the South Coast Air Quality Management District, Los Angeles, California, June 1988.

Betts, Julian R., "Is There a Link Between School Inputs and Earnings? Fresh Scrutiny of an Old Literature," in Gary Burtless, ed., *Does Money Matter? The Effect of School Resources on Student Achievement and Adult Success*, Brookings Institution, Washington, D.C., 1996.

Betts, Julian R., and Robert W. Fairlie, *Does Immigration Induce "Native Flight" from Public Schools into Private Schools?* University of California, San Diego, September 1998.

Betts, Julian, Anne Danenberg, and Kim Rueben, *Equal Resources, Equal Outcomes? The Distribution of School Resources and Student Achievement in California*, Public Policy Institute of California, San Francisco, California, 2000.

Binder, David, Michael H. Shapiro, William T. Rintala, Harold W. Horowitz, and Sidney M. Wolinsky, *John Serrano, Jr., et al., v. Ivy Baker Priest, Appeal from the Superior Court of Los Angeles County, Petition for Hearing in the Supreme Court*, filed October 15, 1970.

Black, Sandra E., "Do Better Schools Matter? Parental Valuation of Elementary Education," Federal Reserve Bank of New York, Research Paper #9729, New York, September 1997.

Blomquist, Glenn C., Mark C. Berger, and John P. Hoehn, "New Estimates of Quality of Life in Urban Areas," *American Economic Review*, Vol. 78, 1988, pp. 89–107.

Bogart, William T., and Brian A. Cromwell, "How Much Is a Good School District Worth?" *National Tax Journal*, Vol. 50, 1997, pp. 215–232.

Borcherding, Thomas E., and Robert T. Deacon, "The Demand for the Services of Non-Federal Governments," *American Economic Review*, Vol. 62, 1972, pp. 891–906.

Brunner, Eric J., and Jon C. Sonstelie, "Coping with *Serrano*: Private Contributions to California's Public Schools," *Proceedings of the Eighty-Ninth Annual Conference on Taxation, National Tax Association*, 1996, pp. 372–381.

California Commission on Educational Quality, *Report to the Governor*, June 1988.

California Constitution Revision Commission, *Final Report and Recommendations to the Governor and the Legislature,* Sacramento, California, 1996.

California Secretary of State, *Lobbying Expenditures: 1989–90,* Sacramento, California, March 1991.

California State Controller, *Annual Report of Financial Transactions Concerning School Districts of California,* Sacramento, California, various years.

California State Department of Education, *California State Testing Program: 1970–71 Profiles of School District Performance,* Sacramento, California.

California State Department of Education, *A Compilation of School District 1975–76 Revenue Limits Computed Pursuant to Senate Bill 90 and Assembly Bill 1267 by County Superintendents of Schools,* Sacramento, California, 1976.

California State Department of Education, *Impact Upon California School Districts of Senate Bill 90 of 1972 and Assembly Bill 1267 of 1973,* Sacramento, California, 1976.

California State Department of Education, *A Compilation of School District and County 1979–80 Revenue Limits Computed by County Superintendents of Schools Pursuant to Assembly Bill 8, Chapter 282, Statutes of 1979,* Sacramento, California, 1980.

California State Department of Education, *Student Achievement in California Schools: 1979–80 Annual Report,* California State Department of Education, Sacramento, California, 1980.

California State Department of Education, *Student Achievement in California Schools: 1984–85 Annual Report,* California State Department of Education, Sacramento, California, 1985.

California State Department of Education, *Selected Financial and Related Data for California Public Schools: Kindergarten Through Grade Twelve, 1984–85,* Sacramento, California, 1986.

California State Department of Education, *Desegregation Funding Options: A Report to the State Legislature As Requested in the Supplemental Report of the 1990 Budget Act, Item 6110-114-001 and Item 6110-115-001,* Sacramento, California, March 22, 1991.

Campbell, J. R., P. L. Donahue, C. M. Reese, and G. W. Phillips, *NAEP 1994 Reading Report Card for the Nation and the States,* National Center for Education Statistics, Washingotn, D.C., 1996.

Carroll, Stephen J., and Rolla Edward Park, *The Search for Equity in School Finance,* Ballinger Publishing Company, Cambridge, Massachusetts, 1983.

Cassell, Eric, and Robert Mendelsohn, "The Choice of Functional Forms for Hedonic Price Equations," *Journal of Urban Economics,* Vol. 18, 1985, pp. 135–142.

The College Board, *College Bound Seniors: Profile of SAT and Achievement Test Takers,* New York, various states and various years.

Coons, John E., William D. Clune, and Stephen D. Sugarman, *Private Wealth and Public Education,* Harvard University Press, Cambridge, Massachusetts, 1970.

Crone, Theodore M., "Housing Prices and the Quality of Public Schools: What Are We Buying?" *Business Review of the Federal Reserve Bank of Philadelphia,* September/October 1998, pp. 3–14.

Department of Finance, *Report to the Legislature of the Desegregation Cost Review Committee,* Sacramento, California, March 1987.

Doerr, David R. "Capsule History of the California Tax Structure," *Cal-Tax Digest,* various months, 1998.

Donahue, Patricia L., Kristin E. Voelkl, Jay R. Campbell, and John Mazzeo, *NAEP 1998 Reading Report Card for the Nation and the States,* National Center for Education Statistics, Office of Educational Research and Improvement, U.S. Department of Education, Washington, D.C., March 1999.

Downes, Thomas A., "Evaluating the Impact of School Finance Reform on the Provision of Public Education: The California Case," *National Tax Journal,* Vol. 45, No. 4, 1992, pp. 405–419.

Downes, Thomas A., and David N. Figlio, *School Finance Reforms, Tax Limits, and Student Performance: Do Reforms Level-Up or Dumb Down?* Tufts University, Medford, Massachusetts, 1997.

Downes, Thomas A., and Mona P. Shah, "The Effects of School Finance Reforms on the Level and Growth of Per Pupil Expenditures," Discussion Paper 95-05, Department of Economics, Tufts University, Medford, Massachusetts, 1995.

Downes, Thomas A., and David Schoeman, "School Finance Reform and Private School Enrollment: Evidence from California," *Journal of Urban Economics,* Vol. 43, 1998, pp. 481–443.

Downes, Thomas A., Richard F. Dye, and Therese J. McGuire, "Do Limits Matter? Evidence on the Effects of Tax Limitations on Student Performance," *Journal of Urban Economics,* Vol. 43, No. 3, 1998, pp. 401–417.

Dynarski, Mark, and Phillip Gleason, "Using Scholastic Aptitude Test Scores as Indicators of State Educational Performance," *Economics of Education Review,* Vol. 12, No. 3, 1993, pp. 203–211.

Educational Testing Service, *Profile of SAT and Achievement Test Takers,* Princeton, New Jersey, various years.

Elmore, Richard F., and Milbrey W. McLaughlin, *Reform and Retrenchment: The Politics of California School Finance,* Ballinger Publishing Company, Cambridge, Massachusetts, 1982.

Enrich, Peter, "Leaving Equality Behind: New Directions in School Finance Reform," *Vanderbilt Law Review,* Vol. 48, 1995.

Evans, William N., Shelia Murray, and Robert Schwab, "Schoolhouses, Courthouses, and Statehouses After *Serrano,*" *Journal of Policy Analysis and Management,* Vol. 16, No. 1, 1997, pp. 19–31.

Evans, William N., Shelia Murray, and Robert Schwab, *Public School Spending and Private School Enrollment,* University of Maryland, College Park, Maryland, February 1999.

Figlio, David N., "Did the Tax Revolt Reduce School Performance?" *Journal of Public Economics,* Vol. 65, No. 3, 1997, pp. 245–269.

Fischel, William A.. "How *Serrano* Caused Proposition 13," *Journal of Law and Politics,* Vol. 12, 1996, pp. 607–636.

Fischel, William A., "School Finance Litigation and Property Tax Revolts: How Undermining Local Control Turns Voters Away from Public Education," Lincoln Institute of Land Policy, Working Paper #WP98WF1, Cambridge, Massachusetts, 1998.

Fournier, Gary M., and David W. Rasmussen, "Salaries in Public Education: The Impact of Geographical Cost-of-Living Differentials," *Public Finance Quarterly,* Vol. 14, 1986, pp. 179–198.

Freeman, A. Myrick, III., *The Benefits of Environmental Improvement,* Resources for the Future, Johns Hopkins Press, Baltimore, Maryland, 1979.

Goldfinger, Paul M., *Revenue and Revenue Limits: A Guide to School Finance in California, 1981 Edition,* Star Publishing Company, Belmont, California, 1980.

Goldfinger, Paul M., *Revenue and Limits: A Guide to School Finance in California, 1996 Edition,* School Services of California, Sacramento, California, 1996.

Governor's Budget, Submitted by the Governor to the California Legislature, various years.

Graham, Amy E., and Thomas A. Husted, "Understanding State Variations in SAT Scores," *Economics of Education Review,* Vol. 12, No. 3, 1993, pp. 197–202.

Hall, Ken, and Paul Goldfinger, *The New Charter School Law—Is This What the Legislature Intended?* School Services of California, Sacramento, California, 1999.

Halvorsen, Robert, and Henry O. Pollakowski, "Choice of Functional Form for Hedonic Price Equations," *Journal of Urban Economics,* Vol. 10, 1981, pp. 37–49.

Hanushek, Eric A., "The Economics of Schooling: Production and Efficiency in Public Schools," *Journal of Economic Literature,* Vol. 24, 1986, pp. 1141–1177.

Hanushek, Eric A., "The Impact of Differential Expenditures on School Performance," *Educational Researcher,* Vol. 18, No. 4, 1989, pp. 45–51.

Haurin, Donald R., and David Brasington, "School Quality and Real Housing Prices: Inter- and Intrametropolitan Effects," *Journal of Housing Economics,* Vol. 5, 1996, pp. 351–368.

Hill, Elizabeth G., *A K–12 Master Plan*, Sacramento, California, May 1999

Horowitz, Harold W., "Unseparate But Unequal—The Emerging Fourteenth Amendment Issue in Public School Education," *UCLA Law Review,* Vol. 13, 1966, pp. 1147–1172.

Horowitz, Harold W., and Diana L. Neitring, "Equal Protection Aspects of Inequalities in Public Education and Public Assistance Programs within a State," *UCLA Law Review,* Vol. 15, 1968, pp. 787–816.

Husted, Thomas A., and Lawrence W. Kenny, *Evidence of State Government on Primary and Secondary Education and the Equity-Efficiency Tradeoff,* American University, Washington, D.C., May 1999.

Jud, Donald G., and James M. Watts, "Schools and Housing Values," *Land Economics,* Vol. 57, 1981, pp. 459–470.

Kirst, Michael W., "Coalition Building for School Finance Reform: The Case of California," *Journal of Education Finance,* Vol. 4, 1978, pp. 29–45.

Klarman, Michael, "An Interpretive History of Modern Equal Protection," *Michigan Law Review,* Vol. 90, 1991.

Kurland, Philip B., "The Supreme Court, 1963 Term. Foreword: 'Equal in Origin and Equal in Title to the Legislative and Executive Branches of the Government,'" *Harvard Law Review*, Vol. 78, 1963, pp. 143–176.

Ladd, Helen F., "State Responses to TRA86 Revenue Windfalls: A New Test of the Flypaper Effect," *Journal of Policy Analysis and Management*, Vol. 12, 1993, pp. 82–103.

Legislative Analyst, *Public School Finance*, Five Parts, Sacramento, California, November 12, 1970, through January 12, 1971.

Legislative Analyst, *Analysis of Senate Bill 90*, Sacramento, California, December 26, 1972.

Legislative Analyst's Office, *The Economic Impact Aid Program: A Sunset Review*, Sacramento, California, June 1987.

Legislative Analyst's Office, *Sources and Uses of K–12 Education Funding Growth: 1982–83 through 1991–92*, Sacramento, California, August 21, 1991.

Legislative Analyst's Office, *Reform of Categorical Education Programs: Principles and Recommendations*, Sacramento, California, April 1993.

Legislative Analyst's Office, *Reversing the Property Tax Shift*, Sacramento, California, April 2, 1996.

Legislative Analyst's Office, Department of Education, and Department of Finance, *New Funding Model for Special Education: Final Report*, Sacramento, California, November 1995.

Li, Mingche M., and James H. Brown, "Micro-Neighborhood Externalities and Hedonic Housing Prices," *Land Economics*, Vol. 56, 1980, pp. 125–141.

Little Hoover Commission, *Dollars and Sense: A Simple Approach to School Finance*, Sacramento, California, July 1997.

Manwaring, Robert L., and Steven M. Sheffrin, "Litigation, School Finance Reform and Aggregate Educational Spending," *International Tax and Public Finance,* Vol. 4, 1997, pp. 107–127.

McCurdy, Jack, "School Funding Ruling: A Setback for the Poor?" *Los Angeles Times,* June 30, 1974.

Minorini, Paul A., and Stephen D. Sugarman, "School Finance Litigation in the Name of Educational Equity: Its Evolution, Impact, and Future," in Helen F. Ladd, Rosemary Chalk, and Janet S. Hansen, eds., *Equity and Adequacy in Education Finance: Issues and Perspectives,* National Academy Press, Washington, D.C., 1999.

Mislevy, R. J., "Randomization-Based Inference about Latent Variables from Complex Samples," *Psychometrika,* Vol. 56, 1991, pp. 177–196.

Mockler, John B., and Gerald Hayward, "School Finance in California: Pre-*Serrano* to the Present," *Journal of Educational Finance,* Vol. 4, 1978, pp. 386–401.

Murray, Sheila E., William N. Evans, and Robert M. Schwab, "Education Finance Reform and the Distribution of Education Resources," *American Economic Review,* Vol. 88, September 1998, pp. 789–812.

National Center for Education Statistics, *Historical Trends: State Education Facts 1969 to 1989,* Washington, D.C.

National Center for Education Statistics, *Digest of Education Statistics,* various years, Washington, D.C.

National Center for Education Statistics, "NAEP 1998 Reading Report Card for the Nation and the States," 1999, NCES Website: www.nces.gov.

Nelson, F. Howard, "An Interstate Cost-of-Living Index," *Education Evaluation and Policy Analysis,* Vol. 13, 1991, pp. 103–111.

Nelson, William E., *The Fourteenth Amendment: From Political Principle to Judicial Doctrine,* Harvard University Press, Cambridge, Massachusetts, 1988.

1992 Trial State Assessment Program in Reading Secondary-Use Data File User Guide.

Oates, Wallace E., "The Effects of Property Taxes and Local Public Spending on Property Values: An Empirical Study of Tax Capitalization and the Tiebout Hypothesis," *Journal of Political Economy,* Vol. 77, 1969, pp. 957–971.

Oates, Wallace E., *Fiscal Federalism,* Harcourt Brace Jovanovich, Inc., New York, 1972.

Oaxaca, Ronald L., and Michael R. Ransom, "On Discrimination and the Decomposition of Wage Differentials," *Journal of Econometrics,* Vol. 61, 1994, pp. 5–21.

O'Sullivan, Arthur, Terri A. Sexton, and Steven M. Sheffrin, *Property Taxes and Tax Revolts: The Legacy of Proposition 13,* Cambridge University Press, New York, 1995.

Payton, Jim J., and Walter G. Hack, "Ohio," in Steven D. Gold, David M. Smith, and Stephen B. Lawton, eds., *Public School Finance Programs of the United States and Canada: 1993–94,* The Nelson A. Rockefeller Institute of Government, Albany, New York, 1995.

Picus, Lawrence O., "Cadillacs or Chevrolets? The Evolution of State Control over School Finance in California," *Journal of Education Finance,* Vol. 17, 1991a, pp. 33–59.

Picus, Lawrence O., "Incentive Funding Programs and School District Response: California and Senate Bill 813," *Education Evaluation and Policy Analysis,* Vol. 13, No. 3, 1991b, pp. 289–308.

Picus, Lawrence O., Allan Odden, and Lori Kim, "California," in Steven D. Gold, David M. Smith, Stephen B. Lawton, and Andrea C. Hyary, eds., *Public School Finance Programs of the United States and Canada: 1990–91,* American Education Finance Association and Center for the Study of the States, State University of New York, 1992.

Policy Analysis for California Education, *Rebuilding Education in the Golden State: A Plan for California's Schools,* School of Education, University of California, Berkeley, April 1995.

Poterba, James M., "Demographic Structure and the Political Economy of Public Education," *Journal of Policy Analysis and Management,* Vol. 16, No. 1, 1997, pp. 48–66.

Reed, Deborah, Melissa Glenn Haber, and Laura Mameesh, *The Distribution of Income in California,* Public Policy Institute of California, San Francisco, California, 1996.

Reese, Clyde M., Karen E. Miller, John Mazzeo, and John A. Dossey, *NAEP 1996 Mathematics Report Card for the Nation and the States: Findings from the National Assessment of Educational Progress,* National Center for Education Statistics, Office of Educational Research and Improvement, U.S. Department of Education, Washington, D.C., 1997.

Reinhard, Raymond M., "Estimating Property Tax Capitalization: A Further Comment," *Journal of Political Economy,* Vol. 89, 1981, pp. 1251–1260.

Reinhard, Raymond M., "When Worlds Collide," *Journal of the California Association of School Business Officials,* Vol. 52, 1987, pp. 23–24.

Reinhold, Robert, "John Serrano Jr., et al., and School Tax Equality," *New York Times,* Education Supplement, January 10, 1972.

Roback, Jennifer, "Wages, Rents, and the Quality of Life," *Journal of Political Economy,* Vol. 90, 1982, pp. 1257–1278.

Rogers, Alfred M., et al., *1990 Trial State Assessment Secondary-Use Data File User Guide,* Educational Testing Service, Princeton, New Jersey, 1992.

Rosen, Sherwin, "Hedonic Prices and Implicit Markets: Product Differentiation in Pure Competition," *Journal of Political Economy,* Vol. 82, 1974, pp. 34–55.

Rubin, D. B., *Multiple Imputation for Nonresponse in Surveys,* John Wiley & Sons, New York, 1987.

Rubinfeld, Daniel L., "California Fiscal Federalism: A School Finance Perspective," in Bruce E. Cain and Roger G. Noll, eds., *Constitutional*

Reform in California: Making State Government More Effective and Responsive, Institute of Governmental Studies Press, University of California, Berkeley, 1995.

Schrag, Peter, *Paradise Lost: California's Experience, America's Future,* University of California Press, Berkeley, 1998.

Serrano, John, Jr., et al. v. Ivy Baker Priest, et al., No. 938254, Superior Court of the State of California for the County of Los Angeles, filed August 23, 1968.

Shires, Michael A., *Patterns in California Government Revenues Since Proposition 13,* Public Policy Institute of California, San Francisco, California, 1999.

Shires, Michael A., John Ellwood, and Mary Sprague, *Has Proposition 13 Delivered? The Changing Tax Burden in California,* Public Policy Institute of California, San Francisco, California, 1998.

Silva, Fabio, and Jon Sonstelie, "Did *Serrano* Cause a Decline in School Spending?" *National Tax Journal,* Vol. 48, 1995, pp. 199–215.

Sonstelie, Jon, "Public School Quality and Private School Enrollment," *National Tax Journal,* Vol. 32, 1979, pp. 343–354.

Sonstelie, Jon C., and Paul R. Portney, "Gross Rents and Market Values: An Empirical Test of the Tiebout Hypothesis," *Journal of Urban Economics,* Vol. 7, 1980, pp. 103–118.

Sonstelie, Jon, "The Welfare Cost of Free Public Schools," *Journal of Political Economy,* Vol. 90, 1982, pp. 749–808.

State of California, *Budget Supplement for Education: 1971–72,* Sacramento, California, 1971.

Sweeney, James P., "The 1987–88 Budget Battle," *California Journal,* Vol. 43, 1987, pp. 446–53.

Tiebout, Charles M., "A Pure Theory of Local Expenditures," *Journal of Political Economy,* Vol. 64, 1956, pp. 416–424.

Timar, Thomas B., "Politics, Policy, and Categorical Aid: New Inequities in California School Finance," *Educational Evaluation and Policy Analysis,* Vol. 16, 1994, pp. 143–160.

Turnbull, Geoffrey K., "The Overspending and Flypaper Effects of Fiscal Illusion: Theory and Empirical Evidence," *Journal of Urban Economics,* Vol. 44, 1998, pp. 1–26.

U.S. Bureau of the Census, *Statistical Abstract of the United States: 1973,* Washington, D.C., 1974.

U.S. Bureau of the Census, *Government Finances,* Washington, D.C., various years

U.S. Bureau of the Census, *Statistical Abstract of the United States: 1994,* Washington, D.C., 1995.

Walden, Michael L., and Craig M. Newmark, "Interstate Variation in Teacher Salaries," *Economics of Education Review,* Vol. 14, 1995, pp. 395–402.

Wells, Amy Stuart, *Beyond the Rhetoric of Charter School Reform: A Study of Ten California School Districts,* University of California, Los Angeles, 1998.

Wise, Arthur E., *Rich Schools, Poor Schools: The Promise of Equal Educational Opportunity,* University of Chicago Press, Illinois, 1967.

About the Authors

JON SONSTELIE

Jon Sonstelie is a professor of economics at the University of California, Santa Barbara. His research interests include several areas in public finance and urban economics, including the effect of public school quality on private school enrollment, the incidence of the property tax, the demand for public school spending, the economics of rationing by waiting, and the effect of transportation innovations on residential locations. He was previously a research fellow at Resources for the Future. He holds a B.A. from Washington State University and a Ph.D. from Northwestern University.

ERIC BRUNNER

Eric Brunner is an assistant professor of economics at San Diego State University. His main research interests are in the areas of public finance, public choice, and the economics of education. He holds a B.A. in economics from the University of Connecticut and an M.A. and Ph.D. in economics from the University of California, Santa Barbara.

KENNETH ARDON

Kenneth Ardon teaches economics at Pomona College. His main research interests are in the area of K–12 education. He holds a B.A. in economics from the University of California, Berkeley, and an M.A. and Ph.D. in economics from the University of California, Santa Barbara.